MW01234542

Broken But Still A Masterpiece

Surviving Multiple Unknown Illnesses

For We Are God's Masterpiece

(Ephesians 2:10)

Broken But Still A Masterpiece

Surviving Multiple Unknown Illnesses

Miyoshi Umeki Gordon

Broken But Still A Masterpiece is the author's attempt to tell her story based on her recollections of events, locales, and conversations. In an attempt to protect others, the names have been changed.

The thoughts and expressions in this book are not necessarily those of the publisher but represent the author.

Unless otherwise noted, all scriptures referenced are from the King James Version of the Bible.

Printed in the United States of America

ISBN Paperback: 978-1-951883-31-7

ISBN Hardback: 978-1-951883-32-4

ISBN eBook: 978-1-951883-36-2

Library of Congress Number: 2020917124

For permission requests, please write to the publisher at the address below:

Butterfly Typeface Publishing
PO Box 56193
Little Rock AR 7215

Dedication

To all the people who have inspired me throughout life:

My beloved parents Joseph Gordon and Mary Frances Roper Gordon, who raised me to become the best person I am.

My dearest siblings, for your deep love shown to me and to my vast extended family, including my forefathers.

My circle of strong women, who lifts me up with inspirational encouragement, and to the dedicated men and women who give of their time unselfishly to be servants to others along with myself for unsurmountable worthy causes.

Thank you!

And finally, thank you to my son:

the Greatest Joy of My Life,

who has been my guiding light since his birth.

He is the love of my life and makes me very

proud of all of his accomplishments.

"Do unto others as you would have them do unto you."

Table of Contents

Foreword

Sometimes when you meet a person, you know the two of you will be friends. That's the way it was when I met Miyoshi Umeki Gordon. She is my lifelong friend or, what some younger people would say, my BFF (Best Friend Forever). We met in the mid-eighties when we both worked at a community hospital. She worked in radiology, and I worked in infection control. It didn't take long for our friendship to bond and flourish into a lasting sister relationship. Although we don't live in the same location, I can feel when it's time for us to have our phone check-up session.

We have shared many experiences in life including raising our children, buying houses, divorces, children's graduations, marriages, and the list goes on and on. Through it all, my friend has been steadfast in her concern for my happiness and wellbeing as I have been for hers. Her love and concern expand to those in her family and many friends.

Miyoshi is one of the strongest women I have ever met. She strives for perfection in all she undertakes. When she told me she was going to start a nonprofit organization to help those with myositis, I thought she was just talking out loud.

But today, five years later, being a successful entrepreneur and helping countless people of all ages, races at different stages of their illnesses, I know she was not just talking out loud. There is one thing I must add. It's hard and almost impossible to say "No" to her when she asks you to do something. She asked me to work with the nonprofit as a board member, and of course I couldn't say "No."

She is driven to help others in any way she can. Her strong faith in God provides her strength and guidance to accomplish the goals she sets for herself. This book is an example of how she wants to help others. She is determined to share her experiences so others will know they are not alone in the journey of life and can use their inner strength to improve their lives.

E. Annette Lanier

Foreword

Broken But Still A Masterpiece will take the reader on the author's journey from childhood to adulthood. The reader may find identity in many of the adversities experienced by Miyoshi Umeki Gordon. Through cancer, failed marriages, and a muscle disorder, she finds strength and direction to become an accomplished Clinical Healthcare Provider, Mother, and Chief Operating Officer (CEO) of a successful 501(c)(3) nonprofit organization.

This book peels back the superficial layers of positive and negative experiences of a high school honor student to CEO. These events and how she found direction to maintain her sanity with tireless energy are candidly discussed.

I first met Miyoshi some thirty years ago in a radiology department in North Carolina. I found her to be an exceptional, self-confident individual. When I was asked to provide radiology services in a rural outpatient clinic, Miyoshi was instrumental in the initial startup. It became exceedingly successful.

You can trust that Miyoshi will be genuine, straight forward, and honest as she tells her story in this book. Her faith in the Lord played a vital role in her bounce back from adversity.

Leroy Roberts, Jr. MD, FACR

Acknowledgments

As I reflect back on everything I have done and gone through in my life, this memoir would not have been possible without my strong faith, love, and support from many people.

I would not be who I am today without the solid unconditional love and steady hands from my beloved parents of Joseph Gordon and Mary Frances Roper Gordon. My father passed at an earlier age; however, my mother was the epitome of our legacy which she lived until the gracious age of 86. She was so humble, caring, and loving to each of her children and our vast family. Her spiritual guidance was given to all of her children at an early age. We can repeat exactly what our mother said in our conversations at family gatherings or by just speaking to each other during phone conversations. My mother allowed me the freedom to be who I am and guided me along the way with a wide path to remain steadfast and unmovable. I was the last one to leave home. My mother and I had such a great bond of love. I appreciate the sacrifices she had made for me as far as getting the proper education and becoming a college graduate. I am forever grateful to her for being an instrumental part of who I have become holding onto my faith when storms rage in my life.

My siblings are the best siblings anyone could have. I know each one of my siblings has his/her own personalities because we were given unique qualities, talents, and skills by our Higher Power. I am so blessed to have nine siblings alive and well at this moment. Growing up with them gave me such cherished memories. We always have such a love bond for each other. It is so meaningful for me to be able to call them at a moment notice and have the best conversations, being on the phone for hours. I will always be grateful for the time I had to spend on this earth with my beloved siblings, Roosevelt, Joseph Jr., and our little sister, Bridget Bardot.

There is no way I could have completed my memoir without the incredible, inspirational, motivational, encouraging, and spiritual people I have met along the way. My Radiology Chairperson, Mary Jane Gentry, Ed.D. and Radiology Instructor, Lettie Sutton (B.A.S., RT-R, ARRT) helped me on my journey towards a career in radiology which all began at Fayetteville Technical Community College. They were strict. They ensured that we met every criterion of the program and helped us become the best Radiologic Technologists. During our radiology internships at Cape Fear Valley

Medical Center, we had some tough Senior Radiologic Technologists, Teresa Bullard (RT-R, CT, ARRT) and Rhonda Sprinkle (A.A.S, RT-R, CV, ARRT). These two technologists did not let anyone go left or right. They were true examples of great Senior Radiologic Technologists who wanted us to excel further in our careers as did our Radiology Chairperson and Radiology Instructor.

Thanks to Teresa Thompkins (RT-R, M, ARRT) and Jacqueline E. Carty (RT-R, M, ARRT) who were both instrumental in providing health materials to our non-profit organization.

There are many other Radiologic Technologists whom I worked beside. I am grateful for each of them. We engaged with the Radiologists during this timeframe of our internship. All of them taught us to become better Radiologic Technologists with their constructive criticism. And yes, if certainly you were standing there with them as an intern shaking in your boots, what the next statement would be from them? I enjoyed working with them; however, a few stick out in my mind so sharply because they were harder and tougher with their advice. Still, they meant well. There was Jerry Ellison, (MD, FACR) who when approached in the Radiologist's Reading Room would state, "One Moment Please." That one moment would turn into 10 minutes; however, I knew not to interrupt his interpretation of reading x-rays because no errors could be made. We were speaking of human patients' lives who had their x-ray procedures reports read with accuracy by the radiologists. The patients' physicians had to make a diagnosis for their health from the x-ray report interpretation. George Binder (MD, FACR) taught me to document every little thing via paperwork, email, written notes with times, and date noted. The reason was to cover yourself so you would not have a malpractice suit. This has remained with me my entire life. I am so grateful for this lesson. Leroy Roberts (MD, FACR) had seen something in me which I did not see in myself. He looked to me, at times, to guide and assist him in setting up an outpatient clinic. Dr. Roberts has seen me grow through many stages of my life from Radiologic Technologist to operating a 501(c)(3) nonprofit organization which he serves as Medical Advisory Board Director. Now, he is witnessing me becoming a first-time author.

Working as a Radiologic Technologist Intern, I was able to gain other full-time employment at Cape Fear Valley Medical Center which was quite enriching to my life for 24 years. These people became my other family because I spent more time with them than I did at home. My Radiology

Director, Joyce McColl (B.H.S., RT-R, ARRT) enriched me throughout my radiology career. It was truly rewarding to promote to several positions: Radiologic Technologist, Traffic Control Technologist, Quality Control Director, and Diagnostic Supervisor. I spent most of my years as a Diagnostic Supervisor with an outstanding Radiology Staff from whom I received encouragement to be the best supervisor I could be. I believed in them, and they believed in me while I empowered them to have a meaningful and insurmountable radiology career as well. Gerry Noon (B.H.S., RT-R, QM, ARRT), Quality Control Director, and Patricia Thomas (RT-R, M, ARRT), Traffic Control Technologist, gave me encouragement and had a listening ear when I needed someone.

Relocating to Indianapolis, Indiana, I gained another work family and had the same position as a Team Leader. I sincerely appreciate my Radiology Director, Kathy Holton (RT-R, ARRT), for hiring and including me in her panel of Radiologic Technologists. I had the opportunity to work with them each day. Traci Dewitt (RT-R., CT, ARRT) and Suzanne Stout (M.S.R.S., R.R.A, RT-R, ARRT) always encouraged me, and when we had hectic days, I always told them to remember, "Be Still, And Know That I Am God." Psalm 46:10 NIV

To this day, we recall communicating this same scripture.

I am so thankful to have my home church, Freedom Chapel A.M.E. Zion Church family with now, Pastor Reverend Boyd Johnson and Lady Denise Johnson and during my childhood, Bishop James Glenn and beloved Lady Ruth Glenn. When relocating to Fayetteville, North Carolina, I joined New Bethel A.M.E. Zion Church family with Pastor Reverend Dr. Orlando R. Dowdy and Lady Marie Dowdy remained there before relocating to Indianapolis, where I attended Eastern Star Church family, Senior Pastor Jeffrey A. Johnson Sr. and Lady Sharon A. Johnson. After relocating to Orlando, Florida, I joined Macedonia Missionary Baptist Church family with Pastor Reverend Dr. Willie C Barnes and Lady Anita L. Barnes.

I am currently under the watch care of Faith Assembly of God, Pastor Carl and Lady Alice Stephens.

Thank you to Ardry Melinda Adams, B.S., M.S.A., middle school principal and inspirational friend.

Having a relationship with Jesus Christ has been part of my life from a very young age and by being grounded in my faith, I have had a better intimate walk with God during the Pandemic. It is at this time that my memoir was birthed to be by God.

I am thankful for those persons who God sent into my life who have kept me lifted up since our first encounter. You were with me during the turbulent times in my life. You listened and did not give judgment. I want to thank Sister Nora Woodard, Minister Johnny and Sister Hattie Greene, Deacon Maurice and Evangelist Marie Jenkins, Sister Patrice Knowles, Sister Ann Smith, Sister Carolean Sanders, and Sister Denise Kenon. I also want to thank my "Diva Sisters," Bessie, Phyllis, Vickie, Dallas and Gina. Thank you to my "Dinner Girls" from Indianapolis, Indiana: Suzette, Teresa, Terri, and Theresa. Dear friends Rose, Sharon, Annie, and Joyce, thank you. There are numerous people I would love to name, but you know who you are. Thank you, nonetheless.

My sincere appreciation to Women's Family Law Firm Christina M. Green, Esq Orlando, FL, you were my solid mind when I could not think for myself. Your legal expertise is beyond the greatest I have ever encountered. You gave me solid advice and straightforward talks. As one of your clients, I value you more than you would ever know.

My health has been a priority throughout my journey. While going through these trials and tribulations, my illness, at times, was exacerbated. I knew I had to maintain managing my illnesses. Dr. Allison Haughton-Green (MD, Faap), Metabolic Nutrition and Research in Orlando, FL, is very exceptional at her profession in maintaining the health of her patients. I was referred to her, by my cardiologist, for high cholesterol. Dr. Green placed me on a nutrition program without any supplements and taught me how to eat properly. I have been holding to this lifestyle/diet to maintain being in remission of autoimmune disease.

I am so appreciative of Dr. Loleta Foster Wood, Ph.D. and Licensed Psychologist, Fayetteville, NC as well as Mrs. Pat Trim, LCSW, BCD, Winter Park, FL. They intervened in my healing process with the following techniques: coping with stress, making meaningful contributions to my communities, realizing my full potential is endless and lies within myself, remaining positive throughout the journey of life, connecting with positive people, getting physical activity, and realizing it is okay to seek mental help and to love yourself first. Mental health is very important because it includes my emotional, psychological, and social well-being. I cannot stress enough that mental health is so very important at every stage of your life, from childhood and adolescence through adulthood.

Seeking mental health assistance has taught me to be my authentic self, to live in the moment and to enjoy each day as it comes. For this synopsis, it lies within me, peace, serenity, self-love, and just being me.

Introduction

No matter what challenges you face in life, with the right attitude, you can overcome them. Pray about all things and have faith that God will move in your favor. While I have become a better person, God is still molding me. With God on my side, I am determined to stay focused. Life may present obstacles, but I was not built to break. The flaws I possess serve to strengthen me. I'm so thankful that God is a forgiving God and that He hasn't taken His hands off me. I am committed to giving myself to Him in order to become the person He purposed me to be.

On January 15, 2020, I left my home in which I had lived with my now former husband. I walked out so peaceful and serene. I had already forgiven him. While I was living in the same home with Jacob, legally separated, I prayed to God that our personalities would not collide as much. I knew, at times, a collision was going to occur. God had strengthened me to endure so many trials, tribulations, and heartache. I knew God would not fail me now. Through it all, God had equipped me in meditation on His Word, prayer, and with the right people in my life whom He knew I needed at this time.

In writing my memoir, I hold dear to my heart that my message will assist those persons who are going through challenges in life to know that God's guidance to help them through their hopeless times. With a strong support system, including your clergy, physicians, nutritionist, psychologists, your unwavering love of family, and your circle of inspirational friends, God is equipping you to make it through. What I have learned is not to let my faith waver in any form or fashion because God is the Beholder of ALL Things.

I am determined to become a better person whom God would have me to be. I am a Breast Cancer Survivor, a Myositis Survivor, and an Emotional Abuse Victim; however, I will **never ever give up**. I am always hopeful that all aspects of my life are in constant motion moving towards better authentic living in the now. Being my real self and feeling free to express myself in a meaningful way with no mask while embracing my vulnerabilities will allow me to encourage other persons as I share what I have gone through in life. I want people to know that they can get through similar situations holding true to themselves and who they belong to, God.

What I keep in mind is my integrity and character in which my parents taught me. I was raised to be true to myself, "Do Unto Others As

You Would Have Them Do Unto You" – The Golden Rule.

Going into a new chapter of my life, I know challenges will come up against me; however, I am better equipped by God's grace and mercy to handle the situations at hand with the use of more helpful resources at the reach of my fingertip. The reality is that I am living my authentic life right now. I am at peace and am serene within myself. That was the Master's plan for writing my memoir. Reconnecting with my true self, I came to know that I had greater strengths and a unique gift for writing my memoir. I learned to re-engage myself with positive people who gave me encouragement and inspiration. I rebalanced my life with my passion for hobbies I loved such as scrapbooking, reading, listening to music, going to the beach, and going on vacations. I had to learn to practice self-love, and I know that it was not a selfish act. Learning to say no without feeling guilty and with no excuses for saying no, I practice positive thinking and remove the worry away from my mind. I'm focusing on my passion for helping other people. I had to reflect upon my passion because it was at the point of giving to others without even taking care of myself. With quiet time and reflection during this Pandemic, I have learned through knowledge of wisdom, the acceptance of being true to my authentic self and living in the moment.

I am so grateful and thankful for this past journey because I have learned I was *Broken, But Still A Masterpiece* in the making by God.

Miyoshi Umeki Gordon,

A Voice for the Voiceless

Chapter One: A Cherished Childhood

Family

My parents (Joseph Gordon and Mary Roper Gordon), grandparents (Belton Roper and Hattie McLaughlin Roper) and great grandparent (Carrie Lee Patterson) were the villages that raised me. My childhood was filled with love and treasured memories. I was born in August of 1958 and raised in the small town of Raeford, North Carolina.

Born into a family of thirteen, my mother, who birthed twelve (ten girls and two boys), embraced my half- brother as one of her own. My parents did not display any partiality between their children. Our family was blended with unconditional love that was pure from the heart.

We had family dinners together where we sat around the table, laughed, talked loudly, and had fun expressing ourselves amongst each other. Mother birthed her children closely, and even today, we consider it a blessing to have such a large family.

When I was five, my baby sister died from a heart condition at the age of ten months. It was a sad, devastating, and confusing time for me. As a child, I couldn't completely understand why this happened. My parents were hurt as well and solicited the help of our older siblings to assist in caring for the younger children.

Holidays

Holidays offered the best-treasured memories, especially Christmas. My parents took turns being Santa Claus. As small children, we didn't know the difference.

"Santa is coming! Santa is coming," we would shout on Christmas Eve with excited enthusiasm.

Our home smelled of fresh fruit and homestyle cooking. Mother always baked my favorite cake, grape jelly and coconut frosting.

As children, we would wish for many things, and although we did not get everything on our list, our parents made us so happy on Christmas morning.

"What did you get?" My siblings asked each other as we laughed and tore open our gifts.

As I reflect on those times, I would not change a thing about my childhood or the way our parents and grandparents raised us.

Father

My father died suddenly from a fatal heart attack. It was unbelievable. One morning my parents left home to purchase a new home for our family. Once they reached the realtor's office in Raeford, North Carolina, my mother said my father pulled the car into the drive; then, his head fell backward. She said she had to place her foot on the brake because the car was still in motion. She had no idea what was happening. Immediately, the Emergency Response was called.

When Mother returned home later that morning, she stepped out of the funeral director's car and said to us, "Father is gone."

One of my sisters, a younger brother, my niece (granddaughter raised by my mother), and I were outside. Our grandparents lived across the street. Grandma jumped off the porch and rushed over to all of us. I was 15 and devastated. We all stood huddled together in disbelief.

Mother

Mother had never worked, and with the death of my father, she found herself needing to chart a new direction for her life. Up until my father's passing, her focus and purpose had been her children. Now, she needed to learn new skills.

She studied for her driver's license, passed the test, got herself a car, and began driving. I'm sure it was a skill she already had, but when Father was alive, she didn't need to drive.

I don't remember a day that any of us went hungry before or after my father's passing. However, I do remember the frequent headaches Mother had that forced her to lie down. At the time, I didn't understand why she had so many. Now, I can understand the reality of the situation. Although Mother had my older siblings to help with the younger siblings, it was still an overwhelming task to be the sole caretaker for so many children.

The Village

Once my father passed, Mother was so lost. She had always been a homemaker and took care of her children. Now, she would need to serve as homemaker and provider. Our family was in a state of grieving. Although most of my siblings were married and raising children of their own at the time, they came home too, and we comforted each other to get through this tough time.

Mother continued to be independent. She landed her first job at the Chicken Plant in Lumber Bridge, North Carolina. She worked there for a short period and later relocated to a better job at Croft Metal which was also in Lumber Bridge, North Carolina. Mother seemed to enjoy this job since she had more friends. At first, she was very shy. Eventually, she met a genuine girlfriend, and they began to talk on the telephone frequently. It seemed she was beginning to find new purpose and enjoyment in life that didn't completely revolve around taking care of her family.

Mother loved her children and grandchildren and kept all of us in line with just her voice or silence. That is how parents were back in those days. They demanded respect and commanded authority, not just with their own children but also with the children in the neighborhood. They understood that it truly "takes a village to raise a child."

Choices

In May of 1976, I graduated from high school at the age of 17. I already had a driver's license, and Mother purchased my first car. It was a 1966 Chevrolet Impala, but I was just as elated as if it were a brand new one.

Mother knew I needed a car because she knew of my post-graduation desires that I had expressed many times during my teenage years. My plans were to attend A & T State University in

Greensboro, North Carolina with my best friend, Kay, whom I had known since 8th grade.

Kay and I are still friends today. We have gone through many stages of life including the ups and downs. I have another genuine friend, and together, we have gone through many battles of life. Together, we all have made it with strong faith and determination to know that trouble does not last always.

While I was determined to attend college, Mother wanted me to remain home. She didn't tell me this, but I knew she was still hurting and grieving the loss of our father.

As a compromise, I made the decision to go to Fayetteville Technical Community College in Fayetteville, North Carolina. I enrolled in August 1977 and majored in Radiology.

Volunteerism

Radiology was something I was familiar with already because I had volunteered at McCain Hospital. At the time, this was where most of the tuberculosis patients were taken for treatment. My job, then, was to transport the patients by wheelchair down to the Radiology Department. I had to be sure they (as well as myself) wore a mask. While I was afraid that I would contract the disease, it was more important for me to work hard to make my parents proud of me. I also wanted to be successful in life one day.

Radiology School Graduate

Jay and I carpooled to and from college each day. We traded off each week driving to college to save money on gas. Having someone to speak with was good for me too. It helped me to stay motivated.

I maintained good grades and was blessed to have a great Radiology Director and Instructor as well as Technologists who took the time to mentor me.

There was one technologist in particular with whom working was difficult. However, she too helped to make me the best Radiologic Technologist I could be. I graduated in August 1979 with honors and received the Mallinkrodt Award silver tray given to the student judged all-around outstanding in the Radiology Program.

Graduation from Radiology School was an honor. I was very happy in my life during this time. I was the first of my siblings to graduate from college. I was even hired during my internship and placed in the role of a full-time Radiologic Technologist at Cape Fear Valley Medical Center.

My family was so happy, and I felt so very blessed to have accomplished one of the many goals I had for my life.

My life had meaning and purpose, but unbeknownst to me, real life was just around the corner.

Chapter Two: I Am Who I Am

Realities

One of the realities I faced was that my opportunity to attend college was made possible through my mother's sacrifice. She used funds from my father's social security death benefits to fund my education. I was more than grateful and blessed because of her generosity.

Another reality centered around the benefit of failure. While I continued to live with my mother and she did offer guidance, I was expected to begin making my own decisions. Thankfully, my parents had taught us early on to set goals, and if you fail at one of them, keep trying. They told us that regardless of how many times you fail, you must keep trying and give it your best because failure was simply a part of success. We were encouraged that even if we deviated from a goal for a time, it was alright as long as we didn't give up completely.

Patience

I commuted from Raeford, North Carolina to Fayetteville, North Carolina, each day for work.

Finally, I felt like I was on my way to accomplishing the goals I'd set for my life.

I really enjoyed working as a Radiologic Technologist and was thankful to the Radiology Directors for giving me the opportunity to be employed. I learned so much from the patients by listening to them. Sometimes, even in their silence, you could hear them speak.

I worked alongside other Radiologists and learned from each of them as well. Each day was different in the workplace. We encountered sick patients who were afraid of an unknown diagnosis that may have awaited them. From them, I learned the importance of the saying that "patience is a virtue."

Work Ethic

As my radiology career continued, I accomplished a lot within a short time period. Because of my hard work, passion, and commitment to the Radiology Department and the Health Center as a whole, I was recognized by my Radiology Director. Consequently, I served in several roles and was given multiple responsibilities which I enjoyed.

I performed as a Radiologic Technologist, Traffic Control Technologist, Quality Control Director, and Diagnostic Radiology Supervisor. As a Diagnostic Radiology Supervisor, I enjoyed working with the Radiologic Technologists and the patients. Each day was rewarding to witness the passion expressed by those I supervised both among themselves and most importantly, towards their patients and the patients' caretakers.

Short Term Goals

At the tender age of 18, I had goals for my life. I had a clear vision of the person I wanted to become. I worked hard, saved my money, and in a relatively short period of time, began to achieve my goals. I was able to purchase my first car, an AMC Spirit.

Life was worth living. Every day I went to a job that I loved in a career that I'd chosen. I had a great relationship with my mother. I felt I could talk to her about anything, and she would listen and offer her advice.

I was content.

My job required me to be on call for emergencies or to help work other shifts as needed. I informed my mother that, in a couple of years, I wanted to purchase a mobile home and move closer to work in order to reduce my commute.

Although I gave my mother money to help her with the bills, I saved, and when I turned 20, I purchased my first home. It was a brand-new mobile home. I was so proud of myself. My mother and siblings were also. I moved to Carolina Country where my new mobile home sat on the first lot as you drove into the park.

Priorities

While dating wasn't my main focus, I had been dating my boyfriend since high school. He had a good job and worked extremely hard. We were both driven to want and have more in life. We both knew we wanted to marry one day but understood it was not the right time. I was concentrating on my career and working long hours.

I enjoyed him, especially on the weekends when I was off, but attending my church (Freedom Chapel A.M.E. Zion Church in Raeford, North Carolina) was still a high priority in my life. The morals and values instilled in me as I attended with my mother, siblings, and grandparents would remain with me my entire life. God became (and is) the forefront of my life. I knew even then how important it was to have Him as the center of my life.

I also enjoyed running, eating healthy, and becoming whom I strive to become. My mind was still set on accomplishing the life goals I'd actually written down in a notebook when I was eighteen.

Chapter Three: Dealing with Drug Addiction

The Rise

After the death of my father, I assumed the responsibility of ensuring that Mother was doing well. However, it soon became evident to me that Mother's life had taken on a whole new meaning. She readjusted to life without my father effectively which was demonstrative of her strong faith in God and perseverance in the midst of trials and tribulations. Consequently, she didn't need me as much.

Carefree and single, I began to enjoy my life. I hung out with my girlfriends and actually relished the freedom my life offered. My career was going well as was my relationship with Peter.

Peter and I came from very different cultures. Even still, we truly loved each other.

I loved Peter for who he was. While he was a hard worker, Peter had no interest in college. I tried to persuade him many times, but he always declined while promising me that if we were to marry, he would definitely take care of me. I was disappointed. However, my family seemed to enjoy him, and we all got along just fine.

When Peter asked me to marry him, I told him I needed some time to think it over. He saved his money, and we worked on a plan "just in case" I decided to say "yes" to his proposal.

In 1983, I decided to say "yes" to marriage. I was 25 and thought this was a perfect time to marry. I was convinced that our marriage was beautiful and would last forever.

Peter and I were both hardworking people. After our wedding, my new husband and I were able to enjoy the fruits of our labor. He purchased a new sports car. It was the car of his dreams. Later, I decided I wanted a new car too. We delighted in the fact that we could have these indulgences, continue to save, pay our bills on time, and maintain a great credit history.

Being responsible with credit was something Father preached to us as children. He always said if you didn't have enough money, your credit would help you get what you wanted. He also stressed the importance of using credit wisely.

After a year of marriage, we both decided we wanted a baby. I wasn't getting any younger, and besides both of our careers were going extremely well.

My Son

I became pregnant and worked throughout my entire pregnancy. Our bundle of joy arrived in May of 1985. Our precious, loving son arrived right on the approximate due date. My husband, my entire family, and I were ecstatic.

The delivery had been difficult. I was in labor for 18 hours. When it was finally time to push, the doctor informed me that every time I did, my son's heart rate dropped. So, he decided to perform an emergency C-Section. I was so grateful when Abel, our son was born normal and healthy.

After giving birth, I developed postpartum depression right away. Although I cried tears of joy the instant he was placed in my arms, as the days passed, I continued to cry. But it wasn't due to joy.

My physician explained that some women experienced this on occasion, encouraged me not to worry, and said that it would pass. And in fact, after a couple of days, it did. I still can't tell you why I experienced this. I was a new mom sitting on top of the world over the birth of my baby boy.

Mother came to our home to assist in taking care of our son; due to the C-Section, I could only lift a few pounds and was slowly walking around. My husband took care of most of the chores around the house while my mother assisted me with the baby and made sure I had the proper amount of rest. She knew that I needed it in order to heal properly and quickly. And I did. My mother was definitely a jewel for all her children when they needed assistance.

Our Village

Thankfully, I never had to put Abel in childcare. My siblings and aunt made sure that he was well taken care of, and I paid them just as if I would have an outside facility. I did this because there was no doubt in my mind that he was getting the greatest care possible. Knowing that reduced any worries my husband and I may have had otherwise, we could keep our minds focused on what needed to be done instead of worrying about the level of care our son was getting.

The medical field operates 24/7 and includes on-call schedules. So, in 1989, my husband and I decided to build a ranch style home in Fayetteville, North Carolina, so my commute to work would be an easier trip. Even though my husband had a longer drive into Raeford, North Carolina for his work, he had taken full responsibility for the care of his family.

Life was good, and we met friends in our new neighborhood. We lived in Hawthorne located off Cliffdale Road. One special family there had a girl and a boy. My son clung on to them immediately. They were so genuine and caring. They would even babysit our son anytime we needed them to do so. We would do the same for their children.

We had many gatherings for our friends and family. They were all very enjoyable. Like most large families, we were not perfect, but because of the love we had for each other and the teachings of our parents, we learned to allow love to have a greater priority.

We learned that we could agree to disagree and still love each other unconditionally. This was very important to me. I wanted my son to know this concept even though he was an only child.

A Sudden Change

My husband always had a Christmas Club Savings Account through his employment. Every year, at the beginning of December, Peter withdrew out all of the funds which ensured we had the most enjoyable Christmas. He made sure that each of us received everything on our Christmas wish list. The savings was so large. There was even enough for us to vacation at Walt Disney World in Orlando, Florida.

The first time we went, my son was so excited. After the first trip, my husband and I noticed that at night, our son seemed a bit lonely as he watched TV or read books. We realized it would probably be best if one of my son's cousins went with him. So, in the following years, the same cousin went with us, and our son did seem to enjoy the trip more because he had a playmate.

Life was going great.

Then, I began to notice a change in my husband's behavior. He would become irritable and frustrated at times. It came to a point where I knew we had to discuss whatever was going on. He would just brush it off as nothing and say it was related to work.

I accepted this and didn't think any more about it until I noticed that he stopped depositing all his biweekly salary into our joint bank account.

"What are you doing with the money?" I asked quite disturbed. Both of us had always been accountable to each other about our financial affairs.

"It won't happen again," he promised without giving me a direct answer.

And for a while, it didn't.

However, I had the nagging feeling that he was into something that he shouldn't be because he had begun hanging out with his friends from his old neighborhood who were not doing anything with their lives. They were always kind and cordial to my son and me, but I still had a sense of uneasiness about them. My intuition told me that my husband was into drugs of some type. I could not prove it, so I just dismissed it.

Little did I know this was just the beginning of my husband's full-blown drug addiction.

The Fall

The housing market was booming, and the interest rates were at an all-time low. My husband and I decided to build another home closer to my job. Looking ahead, we also wanted to be in a great school district for our son when he entered high school.

We moved into our new home in Remington Subdivision. Our two-story home was simply beautiful. It was built with our son in mind who would not only have his own bedroom but a room just for his toys as well.

Abel loved his rooms. The rule was that there would be no playing in the other parts of the house. Abel was to play with his toys in his toy room. Our son did an awesome job with these boundaries in place. That was another thing I learned from my parents. We taught our son what was expected of him upfront.

Our son was truly loved by both his grandparents. He would visit them mostly on the weekend because our jobs required many hours of our time.

In 1995, although I was working full-time, I decided I wanted to pursue a bachelor's degree. I had previously obtained an associate's degree. I enrolled in Campbell University, a branch that was stationed in Fort Bragg, North Carolina. I was grateful for this because it was closer than driving on campus to Buies Creek, North Carolina. The shorter drive was a blessing since I was a working mom with a family. Even though I worked full-time and went to school full-time, spending quality time with my family was still very important.

One of the things I enjoyed doing was playing basketball in the front yard with my son. On one such occasion, my husband and I were out playing basketball with our son, and I fell on the ground for no reason. I thought maybe I just stumbled. My husband rushed over to help me up, and we continued to play.

The next day, I wasn't sore from the fall and went to work feeling like my normal self. When I arrived home from work later that afternoon, I drove into the garage and decided to check the mailbox.

I looked up and noticed that the clouds were heavy, and it looked like it was going to storm. I walked briskly towards the mailbox, and before I reached it, the rain began to come down hard.

Turning to run back to the garage, I fell onto the pavement. I knew there was no reason for the fall. I was a runner and knew this was truly abnormal for me.

The Diagnosis

Later that evening at dinner, I explained the fall to my husband and son and informed them that I was going to make an appointment to see my PCP the next morning. I called the physician's office, and they gave me an appointment time to come in that same day. I had previously called my Radiology Director, told them about my incident, and explained that I would be late arriving for work.

Once at the doctor's office, I explained to my physician what happened, and he immediately ordered an Antinuclear Antibody Test (ANA). This was a test to determine if I had an autoimmune disease.

A few days later, my physician called and stated that he'd referred me to Duke University Medical Center (DUMC) because my titer count was high. I immediately received an appointment to go to DUMC.

The lab test was alarming. It felt like my entire world was unraveling. While I waited for the test results, I reflected on all the things I was doing. I had recently re-enrolled in college, worked full-time, and cared for my son and husband. Moreover, I attended church with my family (which was quite a distance from our new home). My plate was full, and there was no room for illness.

I was referred to a Rheumatologist at DUMC. While waiting for my appointment, I continued my normal activities which included cooking dinner for my family. We always ate healthy with the exception of the holidays. During the holidays, there were no healthy meals in sight which was truly a treat.

One day as I was cooking, I squatted down to the bottom cabinet and struggled to get back up. It was then that I knew that something was definitely happening with my body.

I had always been healthy.

Chapter Four: Invisible Disease Polymyositis

Anxiety

I'd just been told that I had a high titer count which meant I may have an autoimmune disease. It was very disturbing for me. I did some preliminary research, but the disease was very widespread. There was no way for me to narrow down which autoimmune disease I had. The unknown only increased my level of anxiety.

As my next doctor's appointment neared, I found myself not only dealing with my illness but facing the truth about my husband. I began to notice that the changes in my husband's behavior were not getting better but instead were getting worse. He continued to be irritable and frustrated. Although he was careful not to express this in front of our son, I noticed, and it was a source of stress for me. My anxiety was high, and I experienced many sleepless nights.

Finally, it was time to head to DUMC for my physician's appointment. While I was anxious for answers, I was simultaneously dreading this time. My husband accompanied me to my appointment. Knowing that I was nervous, he tried everything he could to distract me during the 90-minute drive including talking about our son, listening to music, and trying anything to put my mind at ease.

Just driving up to DUMC was scary and left me feeling uncomfortable. Once we reached our destination, we certainly had to ask for directions, where to park, and the location of patient parking. The guard kindly gave us directions and instructions, and we went on our way. As we approached the Office of Rheumatology, the outpatient lobby was completely full of patients. It was astounding to see so many patients, but I quickly calmed my nerves by reminding myself that there was more than one physician who would be seeing these patients. Even still, it felt like my wait to see the Rheumatologist was taking forever. Realizing it was my first visit, I understood the new patient procedures all too well.

I was finally called back. The routine checks were completed. I had completed and sent my paperwork ahead of time. The medical assistant discussed my medical history with me in length.

My husband remained in the waiting area. I sat in the patient room alone and continued to wait. I was certainly nervous. My level of anxiety was so high; I knew my blood pressure was through the roof.

What was I about to learn about the ANA tests that were done by my primary physician? The results were about to be discussed with me at that very moment.

The Results

My Rheumatologist stepped into the room and introduced herself. She was such a charming, spirited person with whom I was delighted because her bedside manner was impeccable. I knew this from my experience working in the medical field. There was an instant connection between the two of us.

Dr. Alcox went over my medical history in detail, including that of my paternal and maternal parents and began to discuss the Antinuclear Antibody Test (ANA) (autoantibodies produced by a person's immune system that can fail to distinguish between self and non-self) and explained what an autoimmune disease was.

"An autoimmune disease is where your body attacks the good cells of your body," she explained. "What symptoms have you been experiencing?"

I explained the two falls I had, the difficulty rising from a stooping position and the fatigue which I'd blamed on a busy lifestyle that included caring for my son and husband, work, church, college, Mother, extended family, and all else that life entails.

When Dr. Alcox confirmed to me that I had an autoimmune disease (the exact one wouldn't be revealed until further testing), my heart felt like it stopped for a second. I began to cry softly.

"It is better to find out now," she explained in an effort to soothe me. "This way treatment can begin right away to prevent further spread of the disease."

She went on to explain in detail about the Prednisone I would need to take and the side effects of the medication (good and not so good). At this point, I felt my life had crumbled right in front of me, and I continued to cry.

"You're going to be alright," she assured me. "You've come to the right place for treatment."

After our consultation and more lab work, I checked out and made my next appointment to come back in two weeks. There was an extensive blood panel done and Dr. Alcox would be communicating with me by mail and phone calls since the drive to DUMC for me was 90 minutes.

As I left the hospital, my emotions were overwhelming, and my mind was all over the place. I felt the full weight of my responsibilities, and I began to question God.

"Oh God, why me," I cried. "I am only 37-years-old."

I walked back into the lobby where my husband had been waiting. He could tell I'd been crying. He got up out of his chair and gave me a big bear hug. And before I could explain what the Rheumatologist had said, he told me that everything was going to be all right.

Semblance of Normalcy

I found I didn't want to talk about what I'd learned from the Rheumatologist. I wanted what my husband said to be true. I wanted our life to be normal like it had been. I decided I would tell him what she'd said once I got the final lab results in a couple of days.

Instead, I simply told him I would have to come back in two weeks for the results of today's lab work, and at that time, she wanted to see how I was doing and if I had any further symptoms.

My husband was concerned about my health. When he found out when my next appointment would be, he agreed to take the day off. By the time we drove to DUMC and back, saw the doctor, and ate lunch, it took the entire day. I know he was concerned because I'd never had more than a common cold the entire time we'd been together.

While we waited for the test results, I busied myself with being normal. I came home, cooked dinner, and sat down with my family. Although I plastered a smile on my face, inside I was hurting. I chose not to tell anyone about my hospital visit because I knew they would be worried, especially Mother.

I went to work. I still enjoyed my job and seeing my coworkers. The people I worked with felt like family too; we were that close. It brought me joy seeing patients and caring for them even while I was hurting inside. Determined to keep my routine, I even continued to attend college in the evening. My goal was to complete my degree on schedule.

Betrayal

While all this was going on, I continued to notice the decline in my husband's behavior. He was even more irritable and frustrated and at times even with our son. Sometimes, it was over the simplest of things.

My mind reflected back to when we lived in Hawthorne Subdivision when this type of behavior began. At the time, I dismissed it as him being overly stressed from his job because that was what he'd said. Plus, we were in a good financial state. He had his retirement and savings on his job, as did I, and we had our investments too.

One Friday, I decided to approach him again about his behavior.

"Peter, what is going on?" I was determined to get an answer. "You've been behaving so differently lately. And this isn't the first time I've noticed it."

"Nothing," he said just as I'd expected. "Everything is alright."

To make matters worse, Peter began not coming home on time after work on Fridays. This was odd because Fridays were always our day for family activities.

Both Peter and I had our names on all of our bank accounts. Each of us were paid biweekly and deposited our payroll checks. On one particular

Monday after we were paid, I was checking our checking account as usual and noticed that he hadn't deposited his check into our account. I was perplexed and wondered if it was a bank error or if he hadn't made his deposit. So that evening I asked him about it.

"Peter, what happened to your payroll deposit?"

"I deposited it," he replied.

I thought it made sense to ask him first before inquiring at the bank. I contacted the bank and learned there had not been a deposit made. I was immediately angry. First, I was angry about Peter's dishonesty after I'd asked him directly about the deposit and then the time wasted and embarrassment of chasing a deposit that was never made at the bank only added fuel to the fire.

That same week, I went to Peter's mother's home and informed her of his dishonesty to me. I couldn't understand what was going on. He had never done anything like this since we'd been married.

Neither Peter or I had ever involved our parents in our marriage, but this was one time I had to make an exception. I needed her advice on what to do.

"I think Peter is into something he shouldn't be with a homeboy who lives across the street from me," she said with anger. "I've been seeing his car over there at times and lately it's been more frequent."

"What goes on over there in that house," I asked.

"Drugs," she said simply.

I was so hurt and disappointed because my husband had been living this secret life that he'd kept hidden from our son and me. Peter's mother and I were both overwhelmed with anger and bitter disappointment.

There was also a part of me that felt I should have said something years ago when I first noticed his odd behavior. But I had never known my husband to do any type of drugs, so the thought that he was in this kind of trouble never crossed my mind.

Why Me?

My career was advancing well. I was in college and was scheduled to graduate the following year. I was also in so much pain and hurting over first learning that I had an autoimmune disease and secondly that my husband was addicted to drugs. Life was just not fair. I was working hard, furthering my education, attending church, caring for my mother, being a great mother to my son, and being a great wife to my husband. I loved my family.

So why was this happening to me?

I could not comprehend why my life was suddenly filled with trials and tribulations.

My life was falling apart and all I could do was pray and ask God, "Why me again?"

I had just been diagnosed with an unknown immune disease, and now my life was being hit with another big blow. Although I knew my husband was addicted to drugs, I had no clue what type.

But I was determined to find out.

"Peter, I need to talk to you about your deceitful lies and behavior. I also need to know where your payroll deposit went."

He sat there as if I hadn't said anything, so I continued.

"Peter, I know you're on drugs," I said. "Your mother and I figured it out."

"No," he shook his head vigorously. "I am not an addict."

"You're heading down the wrong path," I said noticing he didn't bother to say he wasn't doing drugs – just that he wasn't an addict. "I can't tolerate a drug addict in my home around my son."

My stress level was severely high. There was tension in our home now on a daily basis. I didn't know if his check would be deposited or not. I knew at this very moment that I had to remain closer to God and my family in this time of need.

Neither of our families or friends knew what was going on. However, one of my sisters told me that her husband heard that my husband was doing cocaine. Like Peter, I was in denial and did not want to believe it or admit it.

However, I knew that my family was never one to meddle in the personal lives of others unless they knew what they were saying was public knowledge.

I chose to remain steadfast mentally, physically, and spiritually because I knew Satan was trying to attack my entire well-being and my family.

Confrontations

My Rheumatologist called me and explained the lab results. She also sent them to me by mail with instructions for my medication. She called into the pharmacy a prescription for me to take 60mg of Prednisone each day until my next appointment which was upcoming that week.

Before heading back to DUMC that week, I finally explained to my husband what I'd learned at my last physician's appointment. He seemed so very sorry about what was happening to my health. Despite his drug use, I knew in my heart that he cared deeply for my son and me.

But there was also a part of me that wondered, *Why are you hurting us by doing drugs?*

I wasn't exposed to drugs of any type growing up, not even as a teenager or as a young adult. My parents shielded us from that. Yet, I knew enough to know that my husband needed professional help if he was going to break this habit.

"You need to get therapy," I told him.

However, he still denied he was even doing drugs.

"I have a lot on my mind, Peter," I said wearily. "And this certainly isn't helping."

At my next Rheumatologist appointment my anxiety level was extremely high as I sat waiting in the lobby to be called by the Medical Assistant. Finally, I was called back, all vitals were taken as usual and then I was led back to the patient room to wait some more.

As I sat there alone, so many thoughts went through my mind.

How will I make it with my son, hold a full-time job, and be a good parent? Will I be able to be a role model for success for him?

My Rheumatologist entered the room with a calm presence. She always knew what to say to make me feel better. We either spoke about my son whom she knew brought me the greatest joy. She asked about his school and sports activities.

Then, we began to discuss my lab results. Based on her demeanor, I knew the news was not good. There were pages and pages of lab results. She explained each of them to me in terms that I would fully understand.

My diagnosis was incurable, Polymyositis and Connective Tissue Disease.

Again, I began to cry softly.

Dr. Rheumatologist knew all about my career and life goals. This disease would derail my plans and send me on an entirely new journey. There would also be challenges as I grew older and the disease progressed.

"You will do well as long as you do your part in regard to your health plan," she explained. "Follow the health plan as recommended."

I promised her I would follow her instructions thoroughly. I wanted to live a vibrant life because of my son. I confessed to her about my personal issues with my husband, and she explained to me that prolonged stress could exacerbate my illness causing it to remain out of remission.

The Health Plan

The goal of my health plan was to get me back into remission immediately and to get my CPK (Creatine Phosphokinase) to return to normal. At present, I had a long way to go. I was placed on 60mg of Prednisone daily and was briefed on the side effects of the medication.

"I'll call you to see how your body is responding to treatment," she promised. "However, if you notice any threatening side effects like inability to breathe or chest pain, please call 911 right away."

Since my commute to DUMC was 90 minutes, my Rheumatologist called to check on me, sent emails, spoke with my Primary Care Physician concerning my diagnosis, and recommended immediate treatment. Thankfully, my Primary Care Physician could see me before my next appointment at DUMC which we had set up on a three-month basis (sooner if needed). Labs were ordered biweekly for a while and later, monthly to monitor the Prednisone dosage.

I felt comfortable with my Rheumatologist's treatment plan and was on board with having my Primary Care Physician involved who was located in Fayetteville, North Carolina and not far from my job. I must admit I felt I was in the best care with both. Working at the Medical Center among other radiologists and physicians was also beneficial to me in case I had questions.

I went on with life as usual believing that my family and I would return to normalcy in spite of my diagnosis and my husband's drug addiction. I was even in denial about the weight gain associated with taking Prednisone. When I began taking the drug, I was only 150 pounds.

"It will only be for a short period of time," I lied to myself. "I know I have to take this now if I want to be healthy."

Unbeknownst to me, I was just getting ready to head into the disaster of my life.

Boundaries

I was so concerned for my son, my health, my career, and the troubling behavior of my husband that I would sometimes get out of my routine of checking our bank accounts. I assumed everything was going well for us financially. I noticed my husband seemed a little disoriented after coming home after work.

Sometimes he would call me to let me know he was stopping by to see his mother who was absolutely fine. When I later discovered he was not telling me the truth about that, I also discovered he had not placed his check in the bank a second time. I hadn't noticed because the bills were paid, and there were no checks returned. I thought our finances were in order as usual.

Peter's drug addiction was getting out of control, and I knew I had to set some boundaries. Again, I immediately discussed with him the things that were stressing me: the care of our son, my illness, college, our financial state, and his drug addiction. And again, he promised me it would not happen and begged me to give him another chance.

I decided to keep the things that were stressing me to myself, including my husband's drug use and financial discrepancies. The sister who told me about my husband's drug use agreed to keep her revelation to herself as well.

I don't know what was more stressful for me, the facts of my life or the attempt to keep them secret. Everyone I came in contact with could see I was gaining weight, but no one asked me about it. I assumed they thought I was pregnant or that life was simply happening to me as it does most people as they age.

Life was happening to me, and finally, I could hold it in no longer. I informed my family and my husband's family about my illness.

My family knew me and how strong I was; they were more worried about if I would continue to be strong (I'm the baby girl of the family). They knew I was in store for a struggle.

I also informed my supervisor because I would need to request time off work intermittently. My boss informed me to complete the Family

Medical Leave forms from Human Resources and have my physician sign where appropriate. I was grateful that I had a very understanding Radiology Director. She knew how important my career was to me.

Chapter Five: Single Parenting

Denial

I was in denial. This was not happening to me.

"This is only going to last a little while," I thought in complete denial. "This is not happening to me." I was convinced this was true. So, I continued on with my day to day activities. Between my career (which was going extremely well) and the greatest joy in my soul Abel, I was able to move forward.

It was time for another appointment at DUMC. Despite the problems in our marriage that stemmed from his drug use, my husband continued to accompany me to relieve some of my fears and anxiety. We enjoyed the 90-minute commute and filled the time with conversations about our son. Abel was the center of our joy in the midst of misery. Because of him, it was important to me to try to remain sane despite the insanity that arose from my crumbling marriage and an invisible illness, Polymyositis.

We reached DUMC on time and went to the office to check-in. I was called back by the Medical Assistant for the routine check-in procedures.

Although I was extremely anxious and tried hard not to reflect it by my mannerisms, it was always shown in my blood pressure. My family had a history of high blood pressure, heart disease, and diabetes.

After my vitals were taken, I was escorted back to the patient room where I sat reading a meditation book which I always carried with me to calm my mind.

My Rheumatologist entered the room with a smile and a kind greeting. She always knew how to put me at ease.

"How's that wonderful son of yours?" She asked and continued to smile.

I brought her up to date on my son and immediately told her about my marriage problems as well. I wanted her to be aware since I was sure that the stress of my home life would probably affect my anxiety level and ultimately my blood pressure. She offered great empathy; then, she guided the conversation to my lab results and the diagnosis of Polymyositis and Connective Tissue Disease.

"How are you tolerating the daily dosage of 60mg of Prednisone?"

"I'm gaining weight," I said, shifting in my chair. "And I feel very uncomfortable. I've always been very conscious of my weight and diet. But regardless of how hard I try, my weight continues to increase. It is very disturbing to me."

I'd always had high self-esteem, but lately, it seemed I was beginning not to feel good with my inner self.

My Rheumatologist was such a wonderful and understanding person. She seemed to know exactly what to say to make me feel like I still was on top of the world.

"Mrs. Gordon," she said evenly. "Even with the added weight, you're still lovely and beautiful inside and out."

This made me smile because at that very moment, I was feeling at my lowest of being a human being.

My Rheumatologist explained to me my lab results were going to be ordered bi-weekly to monitor the CPK levels which were vital in knowing if the disease was progressing or going into remission.

Polymyositis was incurable, and I wondered how I was going to explain this to my son. He needed to be told because the side effects of the medication would become very noticeable.

Prednisone is a corticosteroid drug and is an anti-inflammatory and immune system suppressant. The most common side effects are weight gain, headaches, muscle weakness, moon face, depression, insomnia, mood swings, thinning hair, vomiting, restlessness, loss of potassium, and could potentially interact with other medications that may be prescribed. (www.medicinenet.com)

This wasn't good at all. I had to begin to learn to adapt to my body being a different way. I was no longer in a normalcy stage.

I discussed the Family Leave Forms with my Rheumatologist. She reviewed and signed them. I would then have to return them to my employer's Human Resources Department. The staff there was very understanding and accommodating. It was wonderful. It gave me a great sense of relief to know I would not have any problems on my job taking intermittent time off for my appointments or when my body began to feel so much fatigue that I could not attend work.

Although I was experiencing the side effects of the medication, especially weight gain, I went to work as normal and attended my evening college classes. We were already in the year of 1996. Time was going by so quickly. I had my hands full with family, working, cooking, church activities as well as attending my son's sports activities.

Sportsmanship

Sports were a great teacher for our son. I really enjoyed yelling and screaming for his team to win whether it was baseball, football, or basketball. All the parents were just as excited for their children as we were for our child.

We had to explain to him that it is not how many times you lose, but how many times you get back into the game and play like a winner. He seemed sad once his team lost; however, eventually, he brushed it off and went on with good sportsmanship - just as we and his coaches taught him. After the loss of a game, the coach and his team walked around to the other team and shook hands with each player. We always wanted our son to know we loved him the same whether he won or lost. We were building his self-esteem. This was something my parents taught me and something I wanted to pass on to my son.

At the moment, it felt like I was playing a losing hand. But just as I taught my son to get back in the game and play as a winner, I knew I had to do the same. What helped me was having an attitude of gratitude for the things I had and the things I was accomplishing.

I was scheduled to finish my degree. Somedays, I didn't feel like going to school, but I worked hard "stay in the game." During my last semester, I decided to take a full load of classes (a total of five). I went to class every evening of the week, and each night I returned home fatigued. I had eight weeks to do this, and I was determined to meet my goal.

My husband was taking great care of our son and was cooking for him in the evening. Most Saturdays, we went out to eat at Captain Jerry's Seafood which was a great place to eat. We all seemed to enjoy our family gathering because with my current school schedule, we didn't get to spend as much time together.

Although I wasn't home until 8pm or 9pm most nights, I still had to ensure our son had completed his homework. Sometimes, he would tell his father he had finished his work and my husband assumed our son was telling the truth. If I found out he hadn't, I would get him up out of bed and make him finish in spite of it being his bedtime. This was something my parents instilled in us. We were to work hard, and homework was to be completed as soon as we got home.

I am thankful for my parents and grandparents. We worked hard, but we had fun and enjoyment as well. Grandmother Hattie would have a piece of fatback meat and a homemade biscuit ready for us each day after school. It was a real treat that she knew we would enjoy. My childhood was full of great memories. I wanted that for my son too.

Truth and Promises

As time progressed, I continued to review our bank accounts and realized that money began to leave on a daily basis. I was becoming more frustrated and very angry at my husband about his substance abuse habits.

"If you don't get some therapy and help to get off these drugs, we are going to have to separate," I threatened. "I have enough on my plate with my illness, college, work, and most importantly our son."

"I promise I will change," he insisted.

"I want the money back in the bank account immediately, or you have to leave."

Somehow, he returned the funds to our account, and I thought all was going to go well. I'd set boundaries for our relationship; either he stops using drugs, or he would have to leave. He promised to change, and I accepted his word.

My school and work schedules were quite challenging. I was feeling the side effects of the medication, and in addition to gaining weight, I had sleepless nights, anxiety, hair loss, and mood swings.

My son noticed my weight gain.

"Mother, am I going to have a brother or sister?" He asked innocently.

I was shocked he would even ask me, but I simply replied, "No honey. Mother has gained some weight. I need to exercise more and stop eating so much." I wasn't ready to tell him about my disease yet.

My son wasn't the only one to notice my weight gain. My coworkers noticed, but they didn't ask me directly. They knew I'd always been a very private person concerning my personal life. I did not ask them about their personal lives but encouraged them to do so if they wanted. And sometimes, some of them did.

However, whatever was discussed was always confidential. The only exception was if I had to counsel someone (i.e., a change in work schedule or an issue I could not resolve). Then, my Radiology Director was made aware of their circumstances. I had a great staff to work with, and I tried to be the best supervisor to them in return. This stemmed from the lesson my parents taught us, "Do unto people as you would have them do unto you."

This was great in theory, but there were times (especially in my personal life) that it wasn't as simple as it sounded.

Graduation

It was a few weeks prior to my graduation with a bachelor's degree from Campbell University, and I was in the party planning mood. It was going to be a pool party at our home with great food, family, friends, and coworkers from my job. After all I had been through in my personal life, what I'd done seemed impossible! It was extremely hard most days because my body was becoming more fatigued which was part of the Polymyositis disease.

But certainly, God had been there with me each step of the way.

In August of 1996, I graduated on time. I was experiencing mixed feelings. On the one hand, I was extremely happy that I'd reached my goal, yet my life was drastically changing and not all of the changes were good.

I decided a pity party was not the type of party I wanted to attend. I had worked hard to graduate, and I was not going to allow anything to mar this happy celebration. This party marked a culmination of hard work, dedication, stamina, and enthusiasm. All the people I cared about were in attendance, and I considered them all family. It brought me great joy that they were there to celebrate the fact that I'd weathered the storms. And somehow, I knew that now I could also face whatever was ahead of me as well.

The party went as planned. We had such a great gathering, and to this day, I vividly remember feeling like I was on top of the world. Everyone there was having such a great time. They even brought gifts (which I had not requested). I just loved being around positive people; it brought me so much joy. I smiled, and they smiled. The positive vibes were definitely what I needed in my life at that very moment.

And yes, by the time of my graduation, I was 20 lbs. overweight with a moon face! I chose to make the best of the day regardless of how I felt or looked. I knew that I was my own worst critic as I've always been conscientious of my weight and eating habits.

We had such a grand time, and yes, I did have on a bathing suit. This was my day of celebration! Regardless of all my circumstances, I felt highly favored and blessed. Once the party was over, I gave everyone a sincere appreciation for their attendance as well as their gifts.

Change

I continued my biweekly appointments at DUMC as scheduled. There were no changes or adjustments in my medication. The lab work was done, and I was told I would get the results by mail with appropriate notes.

I eagerly awaited the notes and knew that I would follow the instructions exactly as they were written because I wanted this autoimmune disease to go into remission. I continued to be thankful that I was diagnosed early on, so the disease would not have been so aggressive.

Another thing that did not change was my husband's behavior.

He was still irritable and frustrated almost daily now. And on some days, he still did not come directly home from work. This situation was causing me more stress. He continued to offer false promises, and money continued to leave our bank account without him replacing it. Several times, I had to cover the household expenses.

We had our mortgage, two new cars, credit card bills, and the pool payment. As my parents would say, even all that wasn't the straw that broke the camel's back. That came when my husband failed to pick our son up from after-school care. It was after 6pm, and they called me on my job. I was so angry, and I mean very angry because that was harm to our son. This was beyond poor behavior and irresponsibility in my opinion.

"This was not the same man I married," I said, talking to myself as I drove to get our son.

Once I reached the school, I went to the gym and apologized immediately to the afterschool care teachers. As my son and I walked back to my car, he began to question me.

"Why didn't my Dad pick me up, Mother?"

"I don't know," I said honestly. Usually, my husband called me if he was running late from work.

In my mind, however, I knew exactly where he was.

I immediately called my husband's mother.

"Is your son's car parked at his friend's house?" I asked trying to keep my voice level even.

"Yes," she said.

"Ok, thank you," I said and hung up the phone.

It was important to me not to alarm my son. So, I was careful not to display any anger in front of him. Instead, I asked him about his day, what he had for lunch, and things like that. We always had great conversations because like me, he loves to talk.

When we arrived home, I gave my son a snack while he did his homework, and I prepared dinner. After we ate, my husband still wasn't home.

"Where is my Dad?" I could tell my son was worried.

"Maybe he had an errand to run," I suggested. I never wanted to involve our son in our marriage issues. "Go upstairs and finish your homework. Take your bath and get ready for bed."

I washed the dishes and decided I was definitely waiting for my husband to arrive home. This was it. We would be separating as husband and wife. I could no longer accept his denial of substance abuse or money disappearing from our bank. All of this was too much for me to take on with everything else I was dealing with.

Mental Health

At times, I felt like I was going to lose my mind. But each time I came to that place in my mind, I would put God first. Then, I would think about my only child – a blessing from God without a doubt.

My husband came home that evening at around 8pm.

"What are you doing with your life," I asked. "You are destroying us as a family."

"I promise," he began.

But I wouldn't let him finish.

"No," I said with finality. "You must leave. You forgot our son at afterschool care. You have spent thousands of dollars on God knows what. I have an incurable disease. I can't afford this stress. You need help."

"It's not true," he said but without much conviction. "Please don't do this. I promise you I'll do better."

"I'm filing for legal separation," I informed him. "Once the papers are filed, I'll let you know."

He begged me to change my mind, but I knew this was for the best. Someone who was in denial over substance abuse needed deep therapy to recover. He needed more than I had to give him. My son and my own mental health were at stake.

Although I didn't know much about drug use, I did know that when someone has an addiction, they need to seek help immediately. Addiction is a mental health issue. It isn't as easy as stopping or going "cold turkey." Freedom from cocaine use would only come from my husband going into a drug rehabilitation center.

This man was not the same man I married. This man was sick and an addict.

My husband had been a great man. He worked hard, provided for his family, and paid for vacations and luxuries. You name it; we had it. We were enjoying the fruits of our labor.

Then, Satan intervened.

Satan will kill, steal, and destroy your home and family. It takes two people to do the work to remain together. If one spouse has a clear mind and talks to God, but the other is in denial and unable to accept the truth, there can be no healing or reconciliation. I had to let go and let God because this problem was too big for me to handle. I even offered to attend counseling with him, but he declined.

I had to take care of myself and my son while I allowed my husband to hit rock bottom.

In April of 1997, my husband left our home. Legal separation papers were being drawn up by my attorney. It was no surprise to my husband. He knew he failed, and he also knew he was the only one who could make it right.

By North Carolina law, you must be separated for a year before a divorce can be finalized. I felt this would give my husband ample time to get himself together.

Now, it was just my son and me living in our home. I must admit it was the hardest decision for me to make, but with my husband being a drug addict, it was the only choice I could make.

My family was in total awe over Peter's situation. I was too. We were losing everything we had worked so hard to gain. I had to pray harder, seek peace and comfort through attending church, and lean on family and friends for support. I did not want my job to know about my personal life. I wanted work to still be my happy place where I kept my mind off what was disturbing my inner peace. I not only had to keep my mind clear to take care of my duties and responsibilities at work but also as a mother.

Transitions

At my next DUMC appointment, I informed my Rheumatologist about my husband's refusal to get help for his substance abuse and my decision to legally separate from him. I know the stress from that situation was not helping my disease go into remission.

She advised me to seek counseling for my son and myself.

She also suggested that I inform my Primary Care Physician and that with my consent she would stay in close contact with my PCP as well to discuss the mental health impact on my disease.

Finally, it was time to have the difficult conversation with my son.

Without letting him know that his father was a drug addict, I told him that his mother and father had some differences which needed to be worked out and that his father would be leaving for a while until those problems were resolved.

Of course, my son immediately acted out by throwing his dinner on the formal dining room wall. I knew that he was upset and that this was a shock. I tried to speak gently to him, but the more I did the more unruly he became.

I immediately got his attention when I spanked him all the way upstairs to his room. I was not going to allow him to get out of hand. He was still going to be disciplined. He calmed down after I left his room and later came back downstairs.

"I'm sorry, Mother, for being mean to you," he said softly and embarrassed.

"I accept your apology son," I said, impressed that what he had been taught was rising to the surface. "You have to remember to obey your mother even if your father is not here. Do you understand?"

He nodded his head yes, and we hugged.

The stress of the separation and the added responsibility of being a single parent took its toll. I began to feel more fatigued than usual and had to lie down at times when I didn't want to in order to function.

Abel noticed I was lying down a lot and began to ask questions.

It was time to tell him the truth about my health.

"I have an illness, Abel, that causes me to be more fatigued than usual," I explained. "But don't you worry. I'm going to be alright."

I knew it was important to explain to my son that while some things in our lives would look different, others would remain the same.

"Also," I continued. "We are not moving from our home."

He was happy about that. This neighborhood was our home, and it was also where his friends lived including his best friend, Thomas.

Thomas is also my Godson. His parents, another great family we became fond of, and I all took turns carpooling the children to and from school. Even in the midst of a storm, things were still working out for our good.

Abel and I went to therapy. I went to an Al-Anon support group and set up individual therapy for my son and for myself. I had a strong faith in God but knew that I also needed therapy for my mental health.

Being a "Single Parent" was a transition from marriage. I was now legally separated from my husband, and I did not know what the outcome would be once the year was up.

Would I continue to be married, or would I get divorced?

Chapter Six: My Greatest Sacrifice

Broken

My treatment at DUMC continued. Every three months I was back for lab work and a visit with the Rheumatologist. I could tell the changes in my life (becoming a single parent, legally separating from my husband, living with a chronic illness, and working full-time) were impacting me physically and mentally.

It was almost enough to push me over the edge. I felt so *broken* in more ways than one. My health was failing and so was my marriage. I wanted us to be a great example for my son of what marriage was supposed to be as my parents had been. I married to be married forever according to our vows.

The question, "Why is this happening to me?" was ever-present in my subconscious.

This accumulation of stress prevented me from going into remission.

My Rheumatologist was fully aware of the issues in my personal life because I knew they played a significant factor in the remission process. My visits with her were always positive in a sense; she always had the best bedside manners with me as a patient. She always tried to uplift my spirits by mentioning my son. She knew exactly how I spoke to her about him all the time which brought me joy in the midst of heartache.

My Rheumatologist always explained all treatments and care plans for me. She wanted me to have a great understanding because she knew that my mind would be at ease once I left her until the next three months. My dose of Prednisone was maintained at 60mg, and I was continuing to gain weight along with the moon face. It was a small sacrifice since the medicine was helping my CPK levels to begin to decrease a little.

Diplomacy

My son and I were now living life without a father and husband. My husband was angry with me over the legal separation and was very resistant at the beginning of the process. This was another source of stress for me. I knew it was important for us to come to an amicable agreement for the sake of our son.

It was decided that my husband could see our son with me or his mother present. I insisted on supervised visits because my husband was still not seeking treatment for his substance abuse even though it was recommended by my attorney (He chose not to obtain his own attorney).

At the time of the separation, our son was only 12, and he began to act out because of the changes. Just when he was learning to become his own person, his growth was interrupted by our divorce.

It hurt me so much to see my son hurting and not able to understand fully what was happening between his mother and father. Still insistent on not involving our son in our marital problems, I kept my explanation of the situation as vague as I could. I didn't want to tell him that his father was a drug addict.

"Sometimes, people don't get along," I said trying to remain diplomatic. "They develop differences that need space to resolve." I wanted our son to be free as a child, to continue to enjoy the innocence of being carefree, and to enjoy his peers at his young age.

Abel was a middle school student at Anne Chestnut Middle School. I would drop him off every morning and leave him at afterschool care until my work hours were done. I was thankful afterschool care did not close until 6pm because there were days I had to work longer. Working at the medical center had unpredictable work hours. They operated 24/7, and patients always had to be treated – they had to be a priority. If I had to work past the afterschool closing time, my son went to his Godparents' home.

Normalcy

My son and I continued to live at our home trying to retain some sense of normalcy even though it felt abnormal for his father not to be around.

I was hurting in so many ways.

My illness was still not in remission, and I was concerned about my son's mental health. I wanted him to have fun. He met some children in the neighborhood, and that was great. But they (nor I) could not replace his father.

One family we connected with attended New Bethel A.M.E. Zion Church in Fayetteville, North Carolina which was just around the corner from me. I had attended Freedom Chapel A.M.E. Zion Church my whole life, but now that I was separated from my husband, the drive to and from our home church was too much. I felt overwhelmed. I consulted with my pastor at my home church, and with his blessing, I transferred my membership to New Bethel A.M.E. Zion

Church. It was a wonderful church, and my son really benefited from all the activities they offered. In addition to his mental and social health, I was determined to keep him grounded in his Christian walk with God.

Thankfully, my son had a village to help me during this time. I was comforted knowing his Godparents, Thomas Sr. and Feary McKethan, lived in the neighborhood. They were ready to assist with Abel when I needed them. They were my guardian angels and remain so to this very day.

Although time keeps moving, it is nice to know that there is a solid foundation for people who care about you during good and bad times.

Impacted

Although I continued working full-time, my body was growing weaker by the day. I endured the headaches, muscle aches, sleepless nights, fatigue, moon face, and weight gain. I felt I had to present an outward smile on my face every day, and I had to pretend to be alright in spite of the fact that I was truly hurting with pain on the inside. There were times when my mind was so blurry from fatigue. I literally could not get out of the bed once I arrived home from work. My son knew something was happening to me, and I decided it was easier not to pretend with him.

"Mother is going to be like this sometimes," I explained. "I just need to rest more so I can feel better tomorrow."

And I prayed it would be true. My son would fix himself a sandwich and chips without any hesitation. I kept easy things in the house for him in the pantry, so he was able to feed himself when my body was literally too exhausted to move. I thanked God; my master bedroom suite was on the first floor; however, my son's bedroom was upstairs.

At times on my job, I had to request an intermittent FMLA (Family Medical Leave Act). My Radiology Department Director was so very understanding. There were times I had to call in the morning I was scheduled to work. This is just how devastating the Myositis disease can be; the symptoms come and go without warning. While you are out of remission, your body reacts in many different ways. You have your good days and bad days with no control over what is going to occur. That was the most frustrating part for me because I had to work to pay my bills and to take care of my son.

My husband was still not exhibiting any changes in behavior when we met for him to see our son. Our bank accounts, at this time, were separate. He was ordered to save his funds and to assist me with paying the bills; however, this was not occurring which meant the full financial load fell on me. Not only was I now raising my son on my own, but I was also supporting him financially on my own as well.

I did not want to deprive my son of any sport activities, church activities, or field trips. So, I had to adjust my finances. I sacrificed every way I could (no cable, no going out to dinner, no movies, etc.) I did not have a life of my own. I was living my life for my son. He became my "Greatest Sacrifice." I was determined to ensure he was growing up in a home environment with normalcy, care, empathy, hope, faith, and the full knowledge that I loved him without any doubts.

He would question me at times, asking why his father was not at home. I knew counseling would assist both of us. So, we went to our sessions. His were for a shorter period of time. Children are resilient like that. Once he was with his Godbrothers, he was in his own little world of happiness where he needed to be in his life.

There were times he was grounded for not completing his homework, and it began to occur more frequently. I decided to place him in an afterschool tutoring program. This really assisted him through his junior year of school.

Life as a single parent made the time go by even faster. Before I knew it, the year of separation was nearly over.

I had gotten used to my husband not contributing financially and decided to withdraw funds from my 401k investment. I knew I would have to sustain the early withdrawal penalty, but it was the best course of action at the time. Things had gotten even more stressful due to the financial strain. I contacted my creditors to see if they could lower my payments. Since I was living on just my income, paying the bills was challenging. I desperately wanted to keep my credit in good standing.

Enabling

Although I was beyond stressed, going to work became my safe haven. It was the place I could be genuinely happy. Seeing the faces of my coworkers felt like medicine for my soul. They still had no idea I was separated from my husband.

That is how private I was in my personal life.

There was so much anguish and pain. I could not bear to express it to my family. I knew they would be extremely worried.

The symptoms of my disease and the effects of the Prednisone were creating chaos in my life. The stress prevented me from going into remission.

I kept going to counseling. The counselor was so wonderful. Here was a place I could release myself of all the anguish, pain, frustration, heartache, disappointment, and shock of my life. This was a place I would never believe I would be in my life.

Words can't describe the feelings I had.

I kept asking myself, "Why is this happening?"

My Psychologist helped me to deal with a lot of these feelings. She helped me see that my husband wasn't the only one in denial. I was too. For years, I had been enabling my husband to do the same things. When he promised me over and over again that he would do better, I believed him. That is the insanity of an enabler. I had to learn this in order to begin to love myself.

My Psychologist's sessions saved my mental health and in turned saved my child as well. I had to remain sane for him too. For that, I'm grateful.

Letting Go

The end of the year was quickly approaching, and my husband had not made any changes in his behavior. To me, he was not trustworthy enough for me to take him back as my husband. He was still in denial about his substance abuse.

Christmas came and I made every effort to get everything on my son's *Santa Claus* list. He knew Santa Claus was his parents, but I did not wish to disappoint him. He had been progressing well during his father's departure from our home life.

In April of 1998, the year of separation from my husband was over. I prepared myself as best I could for what was shaping up to be an inevitable divorce. I'm sure my husband knew it too. He had not made any attempt to change even though I'd forewarned him earlier in the year of the consequences.

Together, we decided that it was in the best interest of our son for us to divorce. Neither of us wanted our son exposed to his father's behavior or substance abuse. He continued to deny that he needed therapy to assist him in breaking free from his addiction.

Peter and I met several times before April to discuss how we were going to handle the situation. He allowed me to keep the house and put it in my name with no equity going to him if I ever sold it, in exchange for him not paying child support.

He would get half of the furniture out of our home whenever he chose to. We both agreed for the sake of our son to remain in the vicinity of our home because our son's high school was right across the street from our home.

The agreement was drawn up, and the divorce was finalized in April of 1998.

My prayer was for him to seek therapy, so my son would have a loving father who was drug-free. Peter and I decided we would wait until our son was 18 before telling him that he had a drug addiction.

In the meantime, I covered for Peter. I wanted my son to hear this from his father who I prayed would be clean, sober, and able to explain it to him in his own words. To me, this was important so that my son wouldn't make the same mistakes as his father.

Even though we were divorcing, I wanted to keep some type of normalcy in my son's life. Although his dad wouldn't be living with us, our son would continue to see his father with supervision.

At the forefront of my mind was my son. He remained my "Greatest Sacrifice" through high school and into college.

In order to do this, I knew I had to remain close to God, family, and friends for the support I'd need during what was sure to be challenging times.

I knew my ex-husband would never change until he came out of denial.

As for me, I had to "let go and Let God" give me direction while I lived a single life with a chronic, incurable, and invisible illness that had yet to be in remission.

Photo Gallery

My Beloved Parents

My dearly beloved parents, Joseph Gordon & Mary Frances Roper Gordon, were truly a gift from God. I grew up in a loving environment with 13 siblings in Raeford, North Carolina. We were grounded in spirituality, love, hope, faith, and most of all, to become the best we could be. Our parents taught us to have great integrity and character.

Motto: *"Do Unto Others As You Would Have Them Do Unto You."*

My Beloved Mother

My beloved mother, Mary Frances Gordon, was such a loving, caring, warm, and humble person and a mother who truly believed in God. Her inner strengthen was insurmountable. As I ponder over her life, I remember how graceful she was at living her best and how she sacrificed for her children. She was not only a mother to us but many children in our neighborhood. In the days I grew up the motto, "It takes a village to raise a child." And, that is exactly the way it was. My mother transitioned on March 8, 2010.

Mother was the Legacy of our Family once Father transitioned. She was the true epitome of a strong Christian Black woman. My mother's favorite scripture was Psalm 23.

Photo Credit: *Thomas & Doris Photography*

My Beloved Father

My father was the Provider of our Family. We had great memories of our father. He was brave, a believer, humble, loving, and strong. He showed us what a blended family could be with true love shown to each of his children. During the holidays, especially at Christmas, we had everything on our Santa list. How he and Mom did this, I will never know. "Where there is a will, there is a Way."

He transitioned December June 21, 1974, at a very early age, and I was so heartbroken. However, I will hold on to those cherished memories forever.

A Family That Prays Together, Stays Together.

From the top left: Lillie, Betty, Hattie, Emma, Ruthie, Bernice, Joseph Jr., Bobbie, Doris, Yours Truly, Miyoshi, Sidney, Bridget Bardot, who transitioned at ten months old January 1964.

Forever Thankful & Grateful

Pictured above is our entire blended family to include our brother, Roosevelt McRae (top left). I did not even find out that he was my half-brother until my teenage years because those words were never to be mentioned. There was no partiality shown in our loving blended family. Our parents disciplined us very well, and I am truly thankful from my heart for them keeping true to themselves and their children.

Dearest Siblings & Niece

Granddaughter Twanii; our parents raised from childhood to teenage years. Twanii (fourth) is the daughter of Sister Betty (far left). Our parents had that loving hand in many of our lives.

Siblings not pictured: Hattie, Bernice

Where It All Began

Bottom left: Great Grandmother Carrie Patterson, Grandmother Hattie Roper, Grandfather Belton Roper

Top left: Aunt Dorothy, Aunt Brenda, Uncle William – Children of Grandfather & Grandmother

Great Grandmother Carrie was my Grandmother Hattie's mother.

Uncle John Roper

Son of my beloved grandparents,
Hattie & Belton Roper

Oldest Living Aunt

Maternal Aunt Evelyn Chester (90 years old)

Our Family Home

This is our old home place in which I was raised
with my parents and siblings. The memories will last forever.
I had a wonderful and blessed childhood.

My Cousin

Cousin Viola Gordon McAllister (oldest family member from my father's side of the family)

Author

Me at the sweet age of 6-years-old - priceless

Credit: Upchurch School Photography

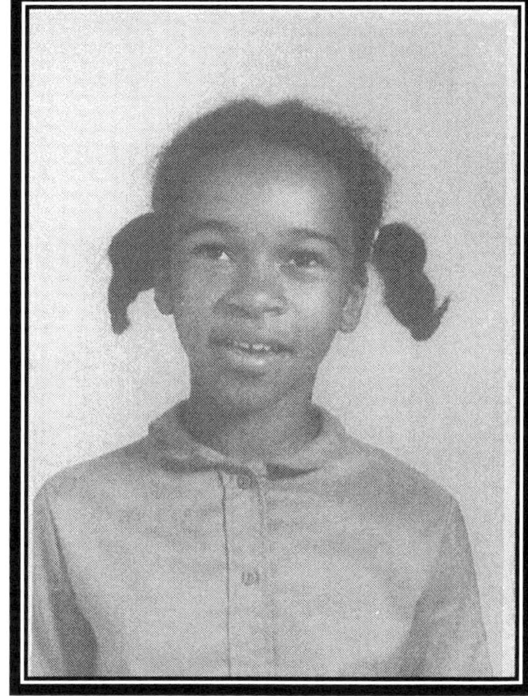

Me at the precious age of 8-years-old.
And I was definitely gazing at the camera.

Credit: *Turlington Elementary School Photography*

Santa Came!

Our Parents had Santa bring us a tricycle
just like this one for my baby brother and me. This was the greatest
treasured Christmas present from Santa.

Credit for Photo: *Unknown*

Author

Hoke High School
Raeford, North Carolina
1976 Graduate
Honors Student
Mascot: Home of the "Bucks"
Photo Credit: Annual Book Hoke High School

Author

I attended Hoke High School in Raeford, North Carolina.

This was my environmental senior picture in 12th grade.

Credit: *Hoke High School Annual Book*

Senior Year Graduate of Hoke High School

Class of 1976 – The Mighty Buck (Mascot)

Served in the French Club, Science Club, Basketball, Library Club, Float, Pep Club, Gospel Choir, Band, Student Council, Senior Council, Senior Executive Board, Student in Action for Education and Senior Hall of Fame.

Credit: *Hoke High School Photography*

Author

Radiology Technology Program
Fayetteville Technical Institute known as Fayetteville Technical Community College Fayetteville, NC

*Graduate of 1979 Honorary Academic & Clinical (Judged all-around outstanding)

*Awarded the Mallinkrodt Award Tray at the Pinning Ceremony

*Achieved Associate of Applied Science Degree

Campbell University

*Achieved Bachelor of Health Science Degree
*Graduate with Honors - Cum Laude

Miyoshi Umeki Gordon,
B.H.S, RT-R, QM (ARRT)

Author Graduation

I graduated from Radiology School from Fayetteville Technical Community College with an Associate of Applied Science in August 1979 and with an honorary in obtaining a silver platter for the Best Clinical Performance Student Radiographer.

Sisterly Love

Sisterly Love – Smiles, Hugs, Laughter, and Fun

Staple Singers Impersonators

Hoke High School Alumni Reunion

Donnie Holmes on guitar - Pop's Staple

Singers Madelyn Miller – Mavis

Karen Brown Floyd- Yvonne

Yours truly Me - Cleotha

CASIO

CASIO

Author

Attended our 40th year Hoke High School Alumni Reunion in 2016.

Chairperson for the Time & Place Committee including obtaining the Event Planner.

Best Friends Forever

Photo Credit: Touch By Serenity

My Best Friend Forever, Karen Brown, "Ride or Die Partner in Crime." I met her in the 8th grade, and the rest is history. We have been through good and tough times in our lives; however, our friendship has remained steadfast throughout our true friendship. I was her Wedding Director in this beautiful photograph. She married Mr. Voneria Floyd.

My Son's Godparents

Thomas, Sr. & Feary McKethan

Thank you for being with me throughout my life journey since we first met each other in our neighborhood, Remington in Fayetteville, North Carolina. You both have been a gift from God for my son and me.

Standing Firm Together

Author, Faith McKinney,
with aspirations and endeavors in 2014 which came to fruition with me during my journey of life.

Photography: *Noyz Production Studios – Ferguson Mayfield*

I launched a 501(c)(3) nonprofit organization in January 2016. UADP Mission is to be an advocacy for Patients and Families with Myositis or Breast Cancer Diseases and Mental Health (Emotional Abuse Victims).

For further information: www.united-adivinepurposeinc.com

Board of Directors:

Miyoshi Gordon, Founder & CEO

Clyde Hough, Asst. President & CFOO

Leroy Roberts, Jr. MD, FACR, Medical Advisor

Deborah McRae, Executive Assistant

Annette Lanier, Board of Director

Tisha Ray, Community Relations Chair

The Sounds of the Ocean

Reminiscing and loving the sounds of the ocean,
which is my safe place.

Galentine's Day

Galentine's Day with the "G not the V" in February 2019

Quote from Emily Bronte

"Ladies Celebrating Ladies"

My 61st Birthday

My 61st Birthday and how well I remember,
my son's job relocated him to Florida. We were eating dinner at The Capital Grille, and my son handed me the letter along with two birthday cards. I opened the long letter first and read it. Immediately, I was literally crying with joy tears. Only God sent me my son back to me in the midst of a life crisis.

No-Diet Zone!

Indulgence in my favorite; a chocolate cake!

Teapot Tea Party

While I am on a journey of life with trials and tribulations, I always have reflections on good memories with my family. I was the last sibling to leave home because I chose to make that sacrifice.

My sister Doris and I enjoyed a tea party with our mother, and we will treasure the little teapots from her tea party still today.

As she grew in older years of living, her children made sure she did not want for anything in life except enjoying the fruits of her labor and unconditional love given by our entire family.

Wonderful Warm Home Memories

Fayetteville, North Carolina

I raised my son as a single parent in this home. There were a lot of sacrifices in my life to maintain this home while raising my son, working fulltime, going to church, attending all his football games, tending to the basic needs of my home, and ensuring my son had the best, especially being disciplined in the proper manner. I wanted my son to succeed in life, and he has far exceeded my expectations.

Blessed & Highly Favored

My two oldest siblings; left Lillie, the oldest sibling 79-years-old and right Hattie second oldest Siblings 78-years-old.

Myositis Awareness

UADP Event at Chuck E Cheese

Myositis Warrior for 25 years

14-Year Breast Cancer Survivor

Supporting Making Strides Orlando Breast Cancer Walk

Lake Eola Park, Orlando FL

What I Know For Sure

I celebrated my 62nd Birthday on August 25, 2020, with the launching of being a first-time author. "Broken But Still A Masterpiece" is the title of my book given to me by the silent whisper of God.

Presently, I am Living my authentic self with peace, serenity, happiness, joy, and a more meaningful purpose: "To Be A Voice For The Voiceless" on breast cancer awareness, myositis awareness, and mental health issues including emotional abuse of both men and women.

By His grace and mercy, I am God's masterpiece still in transformation with an intimate relationship with Him remaining at the forefront of my life.

(Ephesians 2:10 NLT For we are God's masterpiece)

"I Was Broken,

"But Now I Am A Masterpiece."

Chapter Seven: Living One Day at a Time

A New Life

Learning to be a single parent and living with an incurable disease (Myositis) was definitely a time in which I was leaning on God. God, my family, and my church were my network of support. It was so difficult because I did not want to be sick, and I did not want to be a single parent. But life changes, and sometimes and you are given the hardest battles to fight even through no fault of your own.

Of course, at times I was mad at God; however, I know He would not give me these battles if He did not think I was not strong enough to handle them. My faith grew stronger through the challenges. I prayed and prayed because when you cry out to our Father God, He hears us. God may not come when you want Him; however, He is always right on time. It is His will not ours.

I was adapting to single life each day. I definitely had to plan ahead with my son because with Polymyositis, there were some days I could not get up out of bed due to fatigue or muscle aches.

While I was coping with the loss of my marriage, I was also grieving. Grief has no time limit. Grieving the loss of my health and grieving a divorce put a tremendous amount of stress on me. My Psychologist was extremely helpful, and I continued to attend my sessions even if it was after work hours.

The Al-Alon support group meetings assisted me in not being an enabler of any kind and stopping codependence. We shared stories and supported each other. It was a confidential and safe environment. We all were there for a common reason, so we could relate to each other.

Codependency and enabling are common themes for those of us who attended these meetings. Letting go and breaking free of old habits were the goals. Becoming your authentic self was challenging, especially if you were in an unhealthy relationship for a significant amount of time, as was the case for me. I had forgotten who I was before my husband.

A New Business

After the divorce, I had this grand idea to begin a little business called *Sister's Bake & Craft*. My sisters contributed the amount of money needed to complete the launch. Of course, the organization of the business was given to me since I came up with this idea. The business was the cutest little café and shop which offered sandwiches, desserts, and crafts for purchase. We were open from 10:00am-2:00pm. The hours were adjusted to accommodate our customers and the best productive traffic. Revenue and overhead played a huge factor in that decision. I continued to work my full-time job while one of my nieces and one of my siblings operated the business on a daily basis.

My other siblings contributed to the shop by baking cakes and pies. I must say my siblings can really cook very well! These skills were passed on to us by Mother and our grandparents. In the old days, cooking for a big family was the joy of our parents' and grandparents' lives. Gardening was also a big part of our lives and contributed to how healthy we were eating. It was hard work, but with so many children, we were able to divide the tasks among us. Our tasks included chopping weeds from the vegetable garden, picking peas, butter beans, and whatever else was planted. We also shelled the peas and butter beans. Cutting up the collards and mustard greens were left to the older siblings. So, each of us can still cook, and some can even bake. I have always cooked lightly and healthy, except on Thanksgiving and Christmas.

The Sister's Bake & Shop went well for a year; however, due to my health concerns, my sister, who ran the day to day operations, and I had to make a tough decision. I knew that I could not quit my full-time job to operate it because I had to work full-time, take care of my son, and to pay my bills. I had to close the shop which was heart wrenching.

I thought I would have gone completely back in remission or gained some sense of normalcy. However, I continued to struggle each day because of weight gain. I had gained over 60 lbs. at this time and was struggling with low self-esteem because of the way my body looked. I was definitely used to being a size 8 but now was in a size 14 size due to the amount of Prednisone I was taking daily.

Attending my Psychologist's appointments assisted me with my self-esteem, depression, anxiety, and the migraine headaches I was beginning to have. I wondered somedays if I would make it into remission with an incurable Myositis disease.

I constantly prayed and repeated positive words of affirmations like *This too shall pass, Trouble don't last always,* and *Whatever battle God has given me, He has given me the strength to handle.*

Over and over, I told myself, *you're going to make it!*

Dedicated

I would have good days and not good days. This just goes with the Polymyositis disease. A lot of people really do not understand this disease. My family, friends, and coworkers eventually learned I had an autoimmune disease, and everyone was very concerned about my well-being.

Even through these tough times, I was still dedicated and loyal to my employer, church, my son's extracurricular activities, my family, and my friends. I desperately wanted to make life as normal as I could without my husband. I wanted my son to continue to be a child and not to worry about adult issues.

Abel kept me busy, so there wasn't much time for self-pity. It was August of 1999, and he and I were both excited that he'd passed his junior year and was preparing to be a high school senior. I was thankful his school was within walking distance of our home. But beyond the excitement, I was also distressed.

How was I going to handle everything on my own? What about my son's football games? How would

I ensure that he kept up with his homework? Aside from my health, there were so many things to consider.

I had another Rheumatologist's appointment coming up soon which always came with anxiety.

How was I progressing with this disease?

My lab work had been completed a week before, and in addition to talking about that, we talked at length about my plan for my care.

"So, Miyoshi," Dr. Alcox began, "Now that the divorce is final, how are things with you and your son?"

"My son is my greatest joy," I said and smiled genuinely. "I also have a great support system both at home and work."

We chatted a bit more; then, she told me that my CPK levels were not going back down as she would have liked them too and that she recommended a drug called Methotrexate. She also told me that she would begin lowering the Prednisone dose because of the side effects. Weight gain wasn't the only troublesome side effect, but the long-term use of Prednisone tends to reduce bone density and result in osteoporosis.

Dr. Alcox was exceptional with patient care because she cared about her patient's entire wellbeing: physical, mental, and spiritual.

This appointment made me more depressed and more worried about my entire life. I would begin taking the prescribed Methotrexate pills as instructed and was now faced with the side effects from *this* drug which included dizziness, drowsy, headaches, swollen tender gums, mouth sores, hair loss, chills, and fever.

I was also prescribed Zoloft, a depression medication.

I drove home and did not even stop to eat. I just wanted to get home, check on my son, lie down, and rest my mind.

What would be the outcome of all this?

I tried to remain positive and kept repeating, "This Too Shall Pass," and "God Will Not Put More On Me Than I Can Bear." My faith in God was growing stronger and stronger each day because He was the one taking care of me and my son. People say, "Don't worry," but it was easier said than done. However, I chose to focus on the fact that God was with me every step and move I made. There was no doubt in my mind.

Your Best

My career at Cape Fear Valley Medical Center was going extremely well. That was my least worry. My major concerns were my health and the wellbeing of my son. Because I was now a single parent, his responsibilities increased.

I did not involve my son in any of my personal matters, not even in the midst of my divorce. I had never told him his father was a drug addict. That would have been detrimental to a child, and believe me; I was very protective of him in this sense. I wanted my son to be a happy child and to learn from his own mistakes. The only concern I had was his grades in school. I know, for the most part, he was trying; I tried not to be so hard on him. I always had his teachers involved, so if they needed to reach out to me, they immediately could at a moment's notice because his father did not display a major part in his life at this time.

I continued with my counseling sessions because they helped me to deal with life's difficulties. Consequently, I began to deal with my illness better on a day to day basis. I did not dwell on it. I knew what I had to do to maintain being healthy as much as possible. Stress was my biggest hindrance to feeling well emotionally and physically. The lower my stress level, the less fatigue, and muscle pain I experienced.

My Psychologist gave me techniques to use when I felt my level of stress rising. And I would also meditate on God.

Although I was divorced, believe me, I did not even think about dating. I had neither the time nor the interest. My main focus was God, my health, and my son.

Staying busy kept me sane. I did not miss even one of my son's football games the first year - away or home. My son knew I would be in the same section of the stadium home or away side of the bleachers. He would look up as they ran onto the field and look toward my way. There I'd be standing and screaming his name. He would give me a thumbs-up, and that one simple gesture brought me so much happiness inside I just cannot explain. God's mercy and the joy from my son was what I needed to continue to place one foot in front of the other.

I enjoyed his games, whether they won or lost. The first time they lost, my son came home, sat down in the middle of the kitchen and breakfast nook area, and cried like a baby.

"It not about winning all the time," I said, attempting to console him. "It's about playing your best at each game you play. When you give it your best, that is all anyone can ask for."

I wanted my son to believe in himself and to keep believing because I knew that great things were in store for his future.

The Grace of God

With continued Rheumatologist's appointments and medication, I believe I was headed in the right direction with my illness. However, the new drug she prescribed (Methotrexate) was making me sick to my stomach. She lowered the Prednisone dose with each visit, but I was still on depression medication as my anxiety level was high at times. I prayed and prayed because through it all, I knew I had to work for the well-being of keeping my home. I was left with all the credit card bills because my ex-husband was still in denial of his substance abuse.

As I adjusted to my medication, I had to use Family Medical Leave at times. My Radiology Department Director was understanding of this. It was the nature of the disease, and I had to cope with it on a daily basis. Symptoms such as fatigue, nausea, headaches, depression, muscle aches would appear without warning.

One night I was so sick. I had saltine crackers, but I needed some Pepto Bismol and ginger ale. I had to let my son drive to Winn Dixie with only a learner's permit. I knew he was supposed to have an adult in the car, but I felt I had no choice.

"If the police stop you," I said, "Please tell them your mother is sick and needed these items to feel better."

I knew this was against the law, but I was so sick that night. Although the Winn Dixie grocery store was just a couple of miles away from our home, I simply could not make the drive. My son did exactly what I instructed him to do and returned home safely. It was only by the grace of God that my son was able to drive to the store safely without any law enforcement stopping him. Abel grew up much too quickly.

Thanks to my support system that included my son's Godparents, friends, church, and work-family, I was thriving in life. Without the grace of God, I would not have been able to make it from one day to the next.

Around the time of my son's senior year, his father was drug-free, and I was so happy. He went to Pinehurst Substance Rehabilitation Center to become drug-free and stayed there in the center for the full program. It made me very pleased because he wanted his son to see him as a good father. He had already begun to attend his football games the previous year.

I had never told my son about his father's addiction. I treated my ex-husband with respect in front of our son. So, I commended him for becoming drug-free first for himself and for our son and family.

Throughout my son's four years of playing high school football, I worked full time, battled Myositis, and attended all of his games. I love him with all my heart, and I'm very protective of him. I never wanted to disappoint him. As I look back over my life now, I even wonder how I did all that.

It was only God!

My son graduated in 2003. His father began to be in his life full-time because he was drug-free and was thinking more positively about himself and about our son's future. I knew in my heart that one day he would become drug-free and realize the mistakes he made, but it was still overwhelming to see it come to pass.

"I'm so sorry, Miyoshi, for all that I put you through while you were sick," he said.

"For years, I was very angry with you," I acknowledged. "But I had to let it go and be the best mother and father for our son."

I worked hard to care for our son. He never got into any trouble with the law. We had always told him if he went to jail, we wouldn't get him out!

I am so thankful to this very day that he never called our bluff!

In addition to battling the disease and single parenting, I worked so hard to keep my credit score at some level of good. When it dropped to the lower 600s, I decided I needed help.

I went to Consumer Credit Counseling for help with all the credit card debt I'd been left with. I also refinanced my home to lower my payment as I was preparing for my son's college education. I wanted him to continue with his education. All went well with the adjustment of my finances, and I did not even have to file bankruptcy. I certainly did not want to do this because it would affect my credit history for ten years or more.

For the nine years after my divorce, I sacrificed my life to give my son a better life. I thank God I had made it!

A Gentleman Caller

A friend of mine in Fayetteville, North Carolina, did my hair from time to time. We would also have lunch sometimes. She called me one Friday night and asked me to go out to the NCO Club at Fort Bragg.

"Miyoshi, the NCO Club is having an after-hour business party," she said excitedly. "We need to go!"

I really did not want to go. It was Friday night, and I was already lying in my bed.

"No," I said, fatigued from work. "I'm just going to stay home and listen to some music."

"Where's Abel?"

"Abel is at his Godparents' home for a sleepover," I said and immediately knew I'd said too much.

She called me three times trying to change my mind, and finally, I agreed.

"Ok," I said, admitting defeat. "I'll go, but only for an hour."

"That's fine," she said, laughing. "I'll pick you up!"

I threw on a little black dress, some heels, and makeup.

"Remember," I said as I got into her car, "I'm only going for an hour, and I'm only doing this for the sake of our friendship."

I knew she really wanted to go, and I wanted to support her. She had supported me over the years. She was my sounding board. I hadn't dated seriously in nine years, but from time to time, I would accept a dinner invitation with a certain friend.

My son never saw me dating, and I never brought anyone over. I never wanted him to see me as anything other than a good mother. Besides that, in nine years, there had never been anyone I was serious about. Other than dinner and a movie, I didn't have time for anything else.

At the party, this gentleman asked me to dance. I hesitated, but my girlfriend nodded for me to go ahead. He gently took my hand, and we went to the dance floor. After the dance, he walked me back to my table and helped me to sit back in my chair. We exchanged business cards, and that was that.

"Did you call him yet?" Jane asked.

"No," I said calmly. If he is interested, he will call me."

Two weeks later, he did.

"Hello," a strong voice said, "May I speak to Miyoshi?"

"Speaking," I replied. I knew who he was right away.

"Do you remember me? It's Jacob. We met at the NCO Club a few weeks ago."

"Yes," I said, smiling. "I remember you."

We talked for a brief moment, and I found that I did like him. I gave him my cell phone number. He stated he would call me sometime.

I enjoyed the outing, but my main focus remained my health, my work, and my son. I continued to see my Rheumatologist, followed her directions, and saw my Primary Care Physician as well.

My weight was also returning to normal.

Although it was a battle to remain in remission, I was beginning to feel happier.

My son graduated from high school and prepared to go to Fayetteville Technical Community College. He made it in spite of all the trials and tribulations as had I.

God had been so good.

Things were going so well. Was I ready to entertain love again?

Chapter Eight: The Good Life

A Long-Distance Friendship

In August 2003, my son began college. I was still working full time and intermittently using FMLA. Sometimes my body was too fatigued to get out of bed. I continued to attend my doctor appointments in an effort to remain in remission with Polymyositis disease.

It was a struggle, but I managed to hold it together by the grace of God.

I kept my private life private. No one knew I was divorced on my job until my name changed. Then, they wanted to know why I hadn't told them. I reminded them that my job was my happy place, and I didn't want my divorce to interrupt that sanctuary.

Once they knew, they were very thoughtful and caring. They were considerate of the fact that I was now a single parent, working full time and battling an illness.

I smiled in spite of my pain. My faith in God was strong.

Life was going well.

Jacob, the acquaintance I met at the NCO Club, called me again.

"I'll be traveling to Fort Bragg," He said. "Can I call you?"

I told him yes. Now that my son was attending college, I felt like I was ready to begin having a friendship. I had lived my life fully for the love of my son, and now, I was ready for the dating scene.

Although I felt I was ready, I was also apprehensive. I had no idea what dating would look like as a single parent who was very protective of my son. However, I was willing to explore.

Jacob called and asked me to dinner. I happily agreed.

He seemed to be such a wonderful gentleman, very pleasant and caring. He even opened the car door when we went out to dinner. We came to know each other better by calling and chatting on the phone. He lived in Indianapolis at the time, and that was concerning for me.

In my mind, I thought, *how is this long-distance relationship going to work, and I live in Fayetteville, North Carolina?*

"How is this going to work," I asked Jacob one night during one of our long conversations.

"Well," Jacob said slowly. "I think it won't be easy. But with dedication and hard work on both our parts, I think we can make it work."

I agreed. We wanted it to work and were both committed to trying a long-distance friendship first while waiting to see where it went from there.

The Next Level

Despite my illness, I was beginning to enjoy life again. I continued to work, attend church and to enjoy quality time with my son. My Rheumatologist was very pleased with the progression of remission. I'd lost most of the weight I'd gained from the Prednisone and was very pleased with that. Finally, I was able to focus on the positive aspects of life.

Jacob and I were having a good friendship and were moving to the next level of a relationship. We kept in constant contact by phone and when he came to Fort Bragg for work, we enjoyed dinner and spent our evening together. Sometimes he'd have to call it an early night if he had to report back to work early the next morning. I understood work was a major priority. It was that way for me as well.

Once, we decided to go to Myrtle Beach, South Carolina for a weekend where I owned a timeshare. I was very excited. The weekend approached quickly. Before I knew it, it was Friday, and Jacob was in town. He stayed at a hotel that night, and the next morning he came to pick me up.

The day was beautiful. The sky was sunny, the ride was great, and lunch, on the way, was delicious. When we arrived, we decided to sit in some of the white rocking chairs outside of the Community Center. It was so nice just to sit, relax, and have great conversations.

Now that I look back on it, Jacob never had much to say. I did most of the talking. I told him about my hobbies, my job, and my family. Jacob never spoke about his family or how they interacted.

I really enjoyed his company as well as he enjoyed me. We drove back that evening and returned home. When we arrived, he came to my side of the car and opened my door like a gentleman.

He walked me to my front door, and we embraced. He was leaving out the next day.

"Thank you," I said. "I had a wonderful day with you, and I like you a lot."

He smiled. "I'll call you before I depart in the morning."

We wished each other goodnight and safe travel, and he headed back to the hotel.

The next morning Jacob called early.

"Good morning, I like you a lot as well," he blurted out. "Can we begin a committed relationship without dating anyone else?"

"Yes," I said without hesitation. "I am willing to be in a committed relationship, and when the time is right, I will introduce you to my son."

Jacob knew from the beginning about the bond I had with my son. I'd already told him that I would not expose my son to anyone I was dating until I was sure the relationship was going in the right direction. He agreed, and that had really made me more comfortable with a long-distance relationship.

Jacob continued to travel for his job and also to see me on weekends when possible. He was striving to steal my heart, and he did just that!

Responsibility

Life was going well. I was enjoying dating, my job, and attending church. While church could be overwhelming at times (I volunteered with numerous ministries), I somehow managed it all. Only God was the reason I was able to do it all while managing my disease and attending to my son's needs too.

I enjoyed going to church, rejoicing in song, hearing the Word of God, meeting my friends, and having church luncheons. There were so many activities, especially with the youth. My son really enjoyed the youth department, and I was so thankful for all the support I had getting Abel to church and watching over him while I worked.

My job responsibilities were 24/7, and I was grateful to have had a wonderful staff who was helpful and reliable. I was also thankful for my training. When I was an intern during my radiology training, the Radiologic Technologists were tough on me. I did not understand this in the beginning, but after graduation, when I became a full-time Radiologic Technologist, I could understand and appreciate their training because I was well prepared. The Radiology Chairperson and Radiology Instructor were tough and firm. They wanted their students to be the best. Still to this day, I am grateful for them because they ensured their students were successful in their radiology careers and in their advancements in the students' careers.

I applied the same tough learning to my son. With my guidance, I wanted him to be very independent, and he was. He would do his chores, including mowing the lawn on Saturday mornings (which he despised). I wanted him to be responsible. He learned how to iron, cook, maintain his little budget, continue to work while attending college, and attended his college classes as scheduled. He did have some fun time with his friends. He did have a curfew, and if he was not back in on time, he was grounded. This happened one time only. I must admit I was extremely tough on my son. I wanted him to grow up, to do very well in life, and to have a great career like myself.

While I was teaching my son to be responsible, it was something I had to practice as well. In order to remain in remission, I quickly learned I had to listen to my body. Rest was very important. My body told me when I needed it, and it was my job to oblige.

Dr. Alcox taught me so much about the signs and symptoms to watch for and when to slow down to keep myself in remission with the Myositis disease. At times, the Methotrexate drug would make me nauseous and give me stomach pain. My dose was taken on Sundays only, and I had to report for work the next day. So, Mondays were the days I was so sick. However, I managed to work, but if I couldn't, I would take FMLA for the day.

There were times I felt people did not truly understand because "I did not look sick." What a misperception.

During this time, I did take these types of comments personally. People did not truly know how painful it was to me when they thought this way.

And today, I am still dealing with the same stigma: "You don't look sick."

Instead of saying a few choice words I would regret, I choose to say nothing. Ignorance is bliss when you do not have the full details or understanding of something.

There is a responsibility to educate others that I've taken on by sharing my story.

The One

Even through the distance, Jacob and I were still dating strong. There were long-distance phone calls and occasional visits.

In January of 2004, he surprised me.

"Will you go to Hawaii with me?" Jacob asked.

"Hawaii?" I was shocked.

"Yes," Jacob said. "I'll pay for everything."

"Let me think about it," I responded. There was a lot to consider. *What would I do with my son? Could I get time off?* And there was one other very important thing. "There is NOT going to be no hanky panky on this trip."

We laughed about it; however, I was for REAL.

"I'm a gentleman, Miyoshi," he reminded me. "I would not take advantage of a lady such as yourself or anyone else."

I believed him, and within a couple of days, I called him back and accepted his invitation to Hawaii. I was elated he even asked me and even more so that he followed through on the invitation because once I made that statement about no hanky panky, he could have declined the trip.

Jacob immediately booked the flight and a room with two double beds. I was beyond delighted. We were going to the Big Island – Hawaii. This was my dream vacation.

Abel was to stay with his Godparents, Thomas and Feary and his Godbrother. I was very comfortable leaving him with them. I knew they would treat and discipline him just like he was their own child.

Jacob and I left for Hawaii the same week. I met him at the airport in Atlanta. We connected flights into Hawaii which was a nine-hour, nonstop flight.

I was so excited to be going with someone I cared about deeply, but I did not let him know how deeply I felt. This was a test. I wanted to see if he would abide by my "no hanky panky" boundary as we'd discussed.

Our flight arrived safely in Kona. We checked in to a beautiful resort on the Big Island. There was so much to do at the resort. We rode around the Big Island, and it was simply lovely and so relaxing just having a drive down the highways and sightseeing along the way. We would stop and take pictures for great memories.

Each night at the resort, there were always events to attend.

One night, Jacob told me we were going to a luau. I had him explain to me what that was since he'd been before. He also suggested what we should wear. I wore a sleeveless, floral colored dress with beautiful pink, black, and orange colors, simple flat sandals, and a flower in the corner of my hair.

It was such an experience seeing the pig hanging and already cooked knowing that we were going to be eating *that* pig *that* night. There were lots and lots of food and beautiful Hawaiian women to take pictures with before and after their stage performances. The shows were truly outstanding, and I loved Hawaiian music.

The week in Hawaii went by fast.

We explored the resort and shopped inside and outside of the resort. One of my favorite treats was the Hawaiian Host Macadamia nut candy. It was truly a treat. I even bought some back home with me, along with a few souvenirs.

Jacob was a true gentleman on the entire trip and treated me like "Royalty." We had a safe trip back to our separate destinations.

Once we returned home, later that night, Jacob called and talked about the trip. We both decided at this time that we really wanted to be together.

I knew he was the one, but I also knew I had to date him for a year before making any further decisions.

Moving On

I was in the midst of placing my home on the market for sale. Now that Abel was in college, I did not need such a big house any longer. Abel was no longer interested in the pool. He was 18 and was beginning to enjoy college and being out with his friends.

My home was sold in three days. But then the people who placed the earnest deposit down changed their minds. I had packed everything up in boxes was ready to relocate to a condo I was going to rent. They did not wish to purchase my home nor to return the earnest deposit. We went to small claims court, and I won the case and retrieved the funds. I put my home back on the market, and within a week, it was sold. It was very good because my boxes were already packed, and I could still relocate to the condo because no one else had put in an application to rent it. It turns out the owner of the condo was renting it to me. That was only God.

It was finally time to introduce Abel to Jacob.

"How are you, sir," Abel said to Jacob as he reached out his hand to shake Jacob's.

"I'm fine," Jacob said, "How are you?"

"I'm good. I'm good." This was something my son always said.

I smiled, seeing the two men I loved together. It felt like things were going well with the meeting. I was pleased. They continued to talk and laugh. They shared a common interest in football. That made me happy.

Jacob was working down in South Carolina and drove up during an ice storm. The weather was getting better by the time Jacob arrived. I welcomed him inside, and this would be the first time he had an opportunity to see the entire house. In previous visits he had only been invited as far as the formal living room.

If we were going out to dinner, I would let him come inside to greet me; then, we would immediately go out to dinner. When we returned, he would embrace me at the door and depart back to his hotel.

I simply loved my condo in Barton's Landing. It was located in a very private area away from the highway. I continued to work, and Abel attended college.

At my mother's 80th birthday celebration, I decided to introduce Jacob to my family. This was the first time my family had met someone I really cared about. I felt like he was the one for longevity, a relationship, and eventual marriage.

Once Jacob and I stepped into the place where Mother was having her birthday, everyone looked at us in awe. They looked like, *What is going on here?*

I kindly introduced Jacob to my mother.

"You better take care of my baby because she is sick," Mother said.

"I'll take very good care of her," Jacob assured my mother. "I love and care for her from the bottom of my heart."

Jacob was introduced to all my family on this day, and my family is huge. When we had an event for our mother, all the family came because she was the legacy now that our beloved father had gone on to Heaven.

My family seemed to like Jacob. They enjoyed talking with him and made him feel comfortable at the family gathering.

My relationship with Jacob was going well too. He and I were still dating and growing closer. He was getting a little tired of traveling, so we decided I would visit him some time to see Indianapolis because I had not visited this area.

Jacob and I continued to date; however, it was getting a little exhausting with us flying back and forth. He knew I was feeling the same way.

I was on the computer one night reviewing the jobs in the location of Indianapolis came across a job at St. Vincent Indianapolis Hospital for a Team Leader position. It was the same job I was currently doing. I was a Diagnostic Supervisor at Cape Fear Valley Medical Center, which is now Cape Fear Valley Health System. I could not actually believe it.

I called Jacob, and we talked about it. I applied for the position. Jacob and I had previously spoken of marriage, and now, I realized that a proposal would probably happen soon. A week or two went by, and I received a phone call for an interview. I was so elated. I called Jacob to let him know about the interview. It would be conducted via telephone by a panel that included a Radiology Director.

I was so excited; however, the realization set in that moving meant I had to leave my son and my mother, who were both MY HEART.

I had some uncomfortable feelings at this point; however, I went ahead with the phone interview for the job. After having the phone interview, I received a phone call from Human Resources to see if I could fly up to Indianapolis for an in-person interview with the panel and Radiology Director.

I agreed but told them I had to confirm the date because I had to put in a request for a vacation. I figured I'd attend the interview. Then, I would spend some time with Jacob while I was there too.

After my in-person interview with the panel, I felt confident leaving the interview. They informed me that they had other candidates to interview, and Human Resources would contact me either way if I had the job or not.

I had a great time with Jacob in Indianapolis. We went sightseeing, had dinner, and relaxed in his apartment.

Love was truly in the air.

I felt comfortable with him and he the same with me. I flew back home safely and went back to my normal activities. I always had to rest in between because my body would definitely let me know by the signs and symptoms of fatigue.

I had to inform my Radiology Director about the job because I was sure she would be contacted for a reference along with a few radiologists I had placed as references including my Assistant Radiology Director.

I don't think they thought I was serious because before Jacob, I had fallen in love with a gentleman from Atlanta. We'd had a great relationship and were planning to move ahead, but it ended up in heartbreak. I am so glad I did not let my son meet him.

I thought so much of this gentleman; I had his picture on the bookcase in my office.

It turned out that he was dating another lady. I had hired a private investigator and found this out myself. I never told anyone.

It was painful; however, I got through it – again, with strong faith in God.

A New Home

So, this time, I guess the people on my job were having second thoughts about me being in love again.

Thankfully, I live my life for myself and not for people. If people paid my bills, I *might* listen to them, but those who talked knew not to approach me about it.

Anyway, I finally received the phone call from St. Vincent's Human Resources Department to offer me the job. They emailed me the offer letter. As I recall, I had about 3-5 days to respond. I immediately called Jacob to inform him, and he was elated.

However, in the back of my mind, I wondered if I was doing the right thing. I would be leaving my job, my son, my mother, and my family. I had never left North Carolina to live anyplace else.

What a major decision I had to make.

I had to discuss it with my son, tell my Radiology Director, and inform my mother that I was leaving and going to live in the state of Indiana!

After speaking with everyone, I did accept the offer.

Everyone was happy for me. I was beginning a new chapter of my life. I had spoken with my Rheumatologist, and she referred me to one of her co-partners, a Rheumatologist from medical school. I was very satisfied because I knew I really needed to continue essential medical care. I knew once I relocated to Indianapolis, I would find a good Primary Care Physician.

My last day at Cape Fear Valley was a good but sad one. I was leaving a great work family of 24 years and was relocating to a great job as a Team Leader with the same duties and responsibilities. My work family gave me a grand luncheon. It was a very happy time to see I was greatly appreciated during the years I had been employed there. My employer, Cape Fear Valley Medical Center, was a wonderful place during my entire career.

I left full instructions for my son, informed the landlord of my contact information, and said teary goodbyes to my mother, siblings, and the rest of my family.

I knew, from this day forward, I would definitely have to put my life in the hands of the Lord because I was entering into a new life. Only God knew the outcome. I had to lean on him more because I would not have family or my son nearby.

During the next week, I was busy packing my clothes and preparing for the drive up to Indianapolis. Jacob flew down one way, and we drove back to Indianapolis in a snowstorm.

We had to take an alternate route through Atlanta, Georgia instead of through Asheville, North Carolina because the mountains were too risky.

The snowstorm lasted the entire way, as did my tears.

The drive was about 15 hours or more. Jacob tried to console me, but it was just overwhelming to leave my dear son and loving mother. Moreover, I had to get to Indianapolis to report for duty on my new job.

We both were thankful and grateful to God that we made it safely to Indianapolis, which was now my new home.

Chapter Nine: Adjusting to a New Life

The Indiana Weather

It was January 2005. My new life with Jacob and my new job were both going very well. The weather was not nice. The first few days I was there, it snowed. My job was thirty minutes away by the interstate, and I must admit that I hated this weather.

It was nothing like the North Carolina weather. Here, there were four seasons, and fall and winter were the worse. Here, during the winter, there was snow almost every day! My body really did not like it.

I knew I had to contact my Rheumatologist right away to get an appointment because this cold weather was gruesome and brutal for a Myositis disease patient. I had to learn new techniques from my Rheumatologist to remain healthy. I surely did not want to come out of remission.

Jacob had already proposed marriage during the Thanksgiving holiday dinner the previous year while we were in Fayetteville. He had purchased me an absolutely beautiful engagement ring and bridal set. I was extremely pleased with his selection. He chose it all by himself. I would not have relocated if the proposal had not taken place. My job came through so quickly in Indianapolis, and I had to accept it because it was a more income than I actually made at Cape Fear Valley Medical Center. Of course, the cost of living was higher in Indianapolis versus the Fayetteville area.

Jacob and I would do extracurricular activities together on the weekends. We would go sightseeing in Downtown Indianapolis and go out to eat dinner. During the winter months, it really was not a good time to walk around anywhere for me.

Again, I hated that cold weather. I had to learn to prepare more with dressing for the type of weather with additional undergarments. I had to put on extra layers of clothing, so the weather would not feel like it was going through my bones.

Jacob would have dinner cooked by the time I arrived home because his job was only a five-minute drive from our apartment. He was the director of the place where he was employed. He loved his job. Jacob was in the Army and retired as Command Sergeant Major (CSM); although, he continued his employment in Civil Service. He told me that he really enjoyed his military career and that he was enjoying what he does. His career was really successful, and I was very happy for him.

Jacob told me that his first job was as a janitor. Then, he worked as an orderly at a hospital which he disliked. He was from Alabama, and there were no opportunities for young people 17-18 years of age. He had gotten his girlfriend pregnant and decided to marry her. He knew he had to make a better life for his family, so he joined the Army to make a great living for themselves. I felt this was a responsible act for a young man owning his responsibility.

Aside from the weather, I was enjoying living in Indianapolis. Jacob and I were doing well, and my job was going well too.

But I was missing my son and mother so much. At the end of the day, when things slowed down and got quiet, I would cry.

"It's going to be ok, Miyoshi," Jacob would say in an attempt to console me. "I'm going to take great care of you."

I nodded my head and wiped at my tears. I trusted him wholeheartedly. This was the man I was going to be marrying.

The Condo

While I enjoyed our cozy little place, the 5 am train that came by each morning was bothersome. I'm a light sleeper, and any noise will keep me awake. I had to use earplugs. We set the alarm clock on the dresser instead of by the bed because with the noise of the train, we didn't want to risk oversleeping. This way we had to get up to turn it off.

Jacob, of course, was used to it, and he would just laugh about it. However, I did not think it was funny. He also had to have a television (TV) on to fall asleep. In my bedroom back home, during all my years of living alone, there was never a television in the master bedroom. The family room was for watching TV.

My son had a TV in his room, but it was only to play games on when he was allowed to. He had rules and boundaries with his TV until he was about 16 years old. The rule was he would do his homework first; then, he could watch TV for a certain number of hours. If he disobeyed the rules, he knew he would be grounded by getting the car taken away for a week.

Yes, I must admit as a single parent I had to be mother and father to keep him grounded because I wanted him to be responsible and successful in life.

Jacob and I decided to go look for a new place to live. I didn't realize that Jacob had been looking all along. He had more time to do so than me because of my lengthy commute time, and he controlled his own work schedule.

For the most part, I had to report at a certain hour, but sometimes I did not get off right at 4 pm. We had a 7 ½ hour workday where I worked at St. Vincent Indianapolis Hospital. It was a great place to work. It was a faith-based private hospital. The hospital was located on the Westside, and we lived on the Eastside. Overall, I was enjoying my job and my staff, whom I worked with each day.

Jacob and I ended up purchasing a condominium on a golf course. I simply loved the duplex style of the condo. Each condo was one level, and all four condos were attached. We really did not see our neighbors until we were leaving or arriving at home. There was a lot of privacy between the condos in how they were designed. I loved the inside of the condo. It was spacious and airy. There was a sunroom, two bedrooms, two full bathrooms, a bar area with a full kitchen with enough room for a breakfast table as well as a formal dining room and living room. The design was perfect for the two of us.

Once we moved, I was so happy not to hear that train horn blowing at 5 am in the morning. We moved in, and although we were both working full time, in no time at all, we were settled in. Our new place felt like home more so than the apartment where Jacob was living when I relocated to Indianapolis.

Homesick

Jacob introduced me to some of his friends. I did not have close friends at my job which is something I'd never dealt with before. I always kept a business relationship with the people I worked with, with the exception of two female technologists, where I worked at Cape Fear Valley Medical Center. We hung out on the weekends maybe once a month, but we kept it a secret. While we were friends away from the job, I kept it professional at work. They knew I did not play that at all.

That secrecy of a bond as of today is still there. I wish I lived near them, and I miss my entire staff from my past employment.

I still get calls sometimes.

"Ms. Gordon, how are you doing? May I use you as an employment reference?"

I am always so thrilled to hear from them. It makes me feel special that my staff from years ago thinks so much of me as of today. My motto is always, as I was taught as a child by my parents, "Do Unto Others As You Would Have Them Do Unto You." The Golden Rule is something I think we should always remember with whomever you come into contact with.

I began planning our wedding; however, I wanted Jacob's input. But he wanted me to go ahead with the planning and said that we would both take care of the expenses. The wedding was to take place at Fort Bragg in North Carolina. The reception would be at the Officer's Club. Here, I was working full time, decorating our new home, checking in on my son who was in college and trying to plan a long-distance wedding.

Jacob continued to introduce me to his close friends. He wanted to be sure that when he was out of town for work, I had someone to whom I could reach out. I was in a big city with no family. I still cried. I would cry riding with Jacob in the car, turning my head to the passenger side of the window, hoping he would not see the tears. However, he knew I was crying. He would kindly reach over, touch my leg, try to comfort me, and tell me I was going to be alright. I felt so much better when we attended church.

Jacob attended Eastern Star, a megachurch with a pastor who was well known throughout Indianapolis and around the world. His teaching was powerful. He would groom his Associate Pastors and send them out into the community to build their churches. They were a branch from the main church. It was seamless how the pastor had God to use him. I really enjoyed going to the main church because it was not far from our home.

Once church service was over, we would go out to eat at a country place called Mississippi Bell. It really had some good ole country eating like hot water cornbread, sweet potatoes, chicken smothered in gravy, fried chicken, cabbage, and collard greens. You name it; they had it on the menu including homemade desserts.

The owner was a Caucasian man mixed with some other type of ethnicity. However, he was simply the best owner, and his staff worked extremely hard. They served the food in the *ole* country way. They brought it out in bowls of vegetables that you ordered, and the meal was on a push wire cart. Talking about country style, it was simply the best place to eat, and on Sundays right after church, you better be in line there before the line formed out the door. I always loved this place.

On Friday or Saturday during the afternoon, we would go to *Mary's Seafood & Fish*. They had the best whole fish that reminded me of the Carolinas. Her place was small, but you felt like somebody because of the customer service they provided. This was one of my favorite places as well.

Adjusting to all the changes was exhausting. I called my son daily, or he would call me. I missed him and my mother so much. I spent a lot of time in my bedroom crying and praying to God to help me cope. I needed Him now more than ever.

The change of seasons was very evident in Indianapolis. Unlike North Carolina, we experienced all four seasons here; and summer was the shortest season. Thereafter, I dreaded the fall and winter months. It was like I was in hibernation to remain healthy. I seemed to continue to adjust accordingly by wearing the right clothing in the fall and winter. In winter, I felt depressed at times because it was dreary, snowy weather, or snowy, icy weather. Whatever the weather was, I had to work because the hospital operated 24/7. Jacob had the opportunity to remain at home during snow because he was not considered essential personnel.

Living in Indianapolis, I loved the beautiful city, just not the fall and winter weather. It was just too harsh on my body with Myositis disease. I was learning this as the winters went by.

My new Rheumatologist was just as wonderful and caring of her patients as my prior one had been. I thanked God for being referred to her. She kept me in good health. Her major concern was the weather. I'd been diagnosed with Raynaud Phenomenon in my fingers - a condition where the smaller arteries that supply blood to the skin constrict excessively in response to cold, limiting blood supply to the affected areas. (Mayo Clinic and others by Google Search) I had to ensure I wore gloves with furry lining and also in the grocery store when I was reaching into the freezer/refrigerator sections.

Now, more than ever, I knew that Indianapolis's weather was not going to be the best for my Myositis disease. I had to begin to learn more protection techniques to keep my illness in remission. I had made Jacob aware of my illness while we were dating, and my mother had told him directly at her 80th Birthday Celebration while my siblings were listening to see his response. And Jacob responded to my mother, "I will take very good care of her."

My mother was a very wise woman. She had seen something in Jacob which I had not, and I dismissed it. My mother never told us what to do with our lives; she always just advised us in a motherly way.

A Blended Family

As the wedding plans were moving along, Jacob and I got into an argument because I was over budget.

"You do remember that we are flying your immediate family into the Carolinas for the wedding and provide hotel accommodations?" I reminded him.

My family already lived in North Carolina with the exception of my second oldest sister who had no problem attending at her own expense.

I was very upset, and he wanted to call off the wedding. I called his best friends crying, and they came over to our home. I talked to the wife of his friend while he spoke with the husband. I was so hurt and humiliated at this point because I'd made all the plans and paid the deposits.

Looking back, this was definitely a red flag. I was just too blind to see it because of my deep love for Jacob.

Jacob agreed to move forward with the wedding as planned.

I honestly did not know much about Jacob's children because he would only mention them if I asked him about them. His daughter lived in Indianapolis. I remember vividly the day I met her. She came over to our home, and we met her at the back door. Jacob and I were standing there together.

"Hello, Dad," she said but failed to acknowledge me.

I did not say anything. This occurred about twice, and finally, I spoke to Jacob about it.

"Maybe she thinks I am the girlfriend who broke up you and her mother's marriage."

My motherly instinct told me this was probably what was going on. She probably also felt I was taking time away from her that she would have with her father.

"Please speak to her," I said. "I am not the reason for your marriage ending."

I did not know Jacob when he was married. I was in North Carolina and only met him when he was no longer with his former wife.

He said he would talk to her.

This was very important to me. I wanted a blended family with love. In my upbringing with my parents, love and faith were the foundation of our family and still are to this day.

A Warzone

Aside from that one major disagreement, things between Jacob and I were going fine. We continued to work, and on the weekends we did fun things. Jacob was always a great entertainer. We would swing dance in the living room and have some wonderful times. On Sundays, we'd attend church and eat at *The Mississippi Bell* afterward.

Our wedding was set for October 14, 2006, and the day was quickly approaching. There was still so much to be done. My best girlfriend, Kay, was our wedding planner. Kay and I had been friends since middle school. We have a bond that has lasted from then to now.

Kay and I had both experienced our share of ups and downs, but I had no doubt that she would successfully carry out our wedding wishes perfectly. We had phone calls and sent emails each day regarding the status of the vendors, invitations, and whatever else was needed. You name it, Kay handled it properly.

My son was doing well in college; however, he came up with this brilliant idea. He wanted to go overseas, work in logistics, and make tax-free dollars with a contractor for the military in the warzone. My mind left my brain for a moment.

"Son, do you know you are going to be in the warzone, and you could be killed?" I was on the verge of hysterics.

"Yes, Mother," he said calmly, "but I could also die here right at home. When your time is up, your time on earth is up."

I thought about it but remained quiet. I knew what he stated was true; however, this was my only child. My son wanted to go into a warzone. I knew there were many military men and women sacrificing their lives every day to give us freedom in the United States of America. I had to pray hard about this because he would be leaving in November, right after the wedding. I was sad and cried. I had to pray to God to help me cope because I was already overly stressed about planning the wedding. Now, my son wanted to go into a warzone for employment and quit college with one semester to complete.

I must admit my mind was all over the place.

My class reunion was the same year as my wedding. This was great timing because I was able to attend one night of the banquet. We had planned a meeting to finalize the plans at the Officer's Club on Fort Bragg, where the reception was going to be held. We were also meeting with the chaplain for marriage counseling. I really wanted my 2nd marriage to last for a lifetime. I went in with this mindset. I knew, without a doubt, Jacob was the one and only for me.

All the planning went well, and the attendance at my Hoke High Class of 76 Alumni Reunion went well. We impersonated the Staple Singers. We did not have formal rehearsals beforehand. We probably talked for a moment, said what we were going to do, practiced a step or two, got out there in front of our classmates, and had the best times of our lives. Everyone laughed and had fun watching us act the fool. I had to laugh at ourselves.

After the reunion, Jacob and I arrived back home in Indianapolis safely. As usual, it was back to work the next day, and I would be dragging with no energy. After work, I returned home and laid down so my body could catch up on much-needed rest from fatigue.

On many occasions, I felt Jacob did not understand the fatigue I experienced, but instead of discussing it with him, I brushed it off.

Jacob followed up with his family regarding the wedding plans ensuring that everyone was in place and on schedule. He made sure that if they had questions, he answered them.

The Wedding

It was now June 2006, and we were quickly approaching October. The wedding plans were on schedule, but what was foremost on my mind was my son. I was worried about his college education and his plans to work in a warzone.

Finally, I had to give it to God because I was literally worrying myself. I was not able to sleep well. I let go and let God. Peace came upon me. I knew not to do so was not trusting God to take care of him and especially the other military men and women who were already in the warzone. I have strong faith, and it was put through the test right at this time.

When tough times arise, I remember that "This Too Shall Pass."

I was allotted the time off from work for my wedding. I had requested a week if I recall correctly. I knew I needed this time to arrive, make sure all items were in place and to meet with Kay.

Jacob was in charge of checking on the hotel accommodations, the rehearsal venue, and catering. At this point, we were tag-teaming the tasks. Jacob was a big help since he also knew Fort Bragg and many of the soldiers who worked there very well. Many of his prior soldiers remembered him quite well. I am sure it was because he had done extremely well in his military career as CSM. He told me he advanced in a timeframe no one else had. That was definitely a great accomplishment.

The week of the wedding arrived, and we were busy little bees trying to be sure all items were taken care of. My family played a major part in assisting with the planning along with Kay, the wedding planner. Jacob had his groomsmen and best man in order, and I had my matron, maid of honor, and the rest of the wedding party ready. We had approximately 150 people attend our wedding, and for the reception, there were approximately 125 persons.

Our wedding was a dream come true. I felt like a fairy princess. Kay did an exceptional job along with the other wedding assistants. I was extremely happy at this point in my life. My mother and son made it even more special, along with both of our families and friends. By the time the wedding and reception were over, we realized we hadn't eaten.

In our wedding attire, we went for burgers and fries from Miami Grill. We drove up to the drive-through with Jacob in his tuxedo and me in my wedding dress. It was the most hilarious scene you could ever imagine.

"You two just got married," the drive-through employee asked incredulously.

"Yes," Jacob and I said together and laughed. We made jokes while we waited for our food. The employee was very pleasant.

It was smart of us to take the week off because we were both literally exhausted after the wedding. We did not go on a honeymoon at this time. We planned it later, and I was happy that we did. After resting for a while, we returned to the hotel to rest because we had to drive back home to Indianapolis.

The drive was not short. We had so many gifts in the car to unload. I was thankful it was a weekend, so we could take our time to return to Indianapolis.

My son was leaving on November 5th, heading overseas. Again, with mixed emotions, I still would have my moments thinking about my only child going into a warzone. But then I'd remember to let go and let God because worrying was taking a toll on me.

We talked continuously by phone before he departed. He let me know every move he made by calling.

While I was home for the wedding, my son and I had signed the papers for Power of Attorney while he was overseas because I had to handle all his affairs while he was away. His father had agreed to take his cars out for a drive periodically, and my brother-in-law agreed to do it when my son's father could not make it to the storage area.

He called to tell me when they were taking off. He let me know it would be a week or so before I would hear from him. I continued to pray. We kept in touch using the WhatsApp. He kept his phone, but I would suspend his account with no charge until he told me to unsuspend it once he arrived at this destination. I felt so much more comfort in my spirit.

Another Unknown Illness

After the wedding, I remembered that in September, I'd gotten a notice about a need for an additional mammogram. I did not think it was anything that could not wait until after the wedding. Once things settled down, I finally made the appointment to have the extra views done for my mammogram. The results came back on December 5th when I was at work.

I was just stepping into my office at work when one of our radiologists called me.

"Mrs. Gordon?"

"This is Miyoshi."

"Mrs. Gordon, I'm calling to tell you that your mammogram came back positive for breast cancer."

"Are you sure you read my x-rays correctly?" I asked.

"Yes, ma'am," he said clearly. "I'm sure."

"Thank you," I managed to say weakly. I almost fell to the floor.

I sat in a chair quickly, put my head in my hands, and began to sob. Finally, I called one of my senior technologists to tell her the news. She notified my Radiology Director, who was in a meeting.

The Radiology Director's secretary drove me home because Jacob was in a meeting with Senior Executive Service at his job and was heading home thereafter. Since someone was able to bring me, it was good; he did not want me waiting. By the time he arrived, it would have been about 45 minutes or more. I was grateful the secretary was able to take me.

When someone tells you by phone that you have breast cancer, you think you are going to die. However, once the radiology report was reviewed, the cancer was DCIS (Ductal Carcinoma Breast Cancer). I did not have a full understanding of breast cancer.

Anyone can tell you it's nothing to worry about, but it's not them with the diagnosis. I was scared to death. The only thing going through my mind was that I was going to die. I didn't know what was going to happen. I was already dealing with an incurable Myositis disease.

People look at you and have no clue what you're going through. I didn't look like what I was going through. I do plan to talk about it in a later book on a deeper level. I want people to understand exactly what happens.

As I said, I was thankful the secretary brought me home. Soon after I arrived, Jacob came home. He saw me sobbing, and he grabbed me and hugged me tightly.

"How did this happen?" I cried.

Jacob didn't have a clue. He told me to relax and lie down, which I did.

My Primary Care Physician immediately received the radiology report and called me. He referred me to a Breast Surgeon, and I immediately received an appointment the next week. I called my family and my best friend, Kay, to inform them of my diagnosis. Kay's family member had just gone through breast cancer.

"I'm glad you found out," Kay said expertly. "Now, we can do something about it."

"Huh?"

"When my family member found out, she did something right away, and it was the best thing."

My girlfriend always knew what to say and how to calm me down. It was no wonder we had been friends for more than a decade.

I chose not to tell my son since he was in a warzone. I didn't want him worrying or distracted.

I had to go through a needle biopsy on my left breast first for the Breast Surgeon to view the exact location of the cancer. Then, after receiving the results, I had an appointment with her to review the results, and she explained that I would be having a lumpectomy on my left side.

I was quite okay with this part.

She was referring me to a medical oncologist and radiation oncologist as well to have the best options for my complete treatment since I had a Myositis disease. This was a major part of the Team's Care decision. I kept working as normal because it was good to take my mind off things; although, it still was in the back of my mind.

The surgery was scheduled for the first week in January 2007. The surgery went well, and I came home safely. Kay came up to spend a week with me to help Jacob and me. I knew he would be stressed, and he could work when I had Kay with me. One of my family members could have come; however, Kay's schedule was more flexible.

Once I was home recovering, my son called from overseas.

"Mother, are you ok?"

"Yes," I said, but I was so drowsy.

"Is that Aunt Kay's voice I hear in the background?"

"Yes," I said. "Son, she came up for a visit."

"Please tell her I said hello, and I love her for being there with you for a visit."

I knew I could not tell him because he would jump on the next flight and come home.

The next morning, there was a knock at the door. I thought Jacob or Kay would hear the door knock; however, they both were knocked out asleep. I managed to get up. I peeped through the peephole and saw it was a delivery person. I received the plant, dragged it inside, and left it in the entryway.

Later, when Jacob and Kay were awake, they had questions.

"When was this plant delivered?"

"While y'all were sleeping," I said innocently.

We laughed about it. I was the patient, and they were my caretakers.

I laid back down to rest. Jacob and Kay went into the kitchen to cook breakfast. I got up and went to the breakfast table to eat breakfast. I immediately smelled the toast burning with them both in the kitchen.

"The toast is burning," I said.

They rushed to the toaster, but the toast was completely burned.

I laughed so hard.

"Y'all the caretakers," I said, still laughing. "but y'all trying to burn down the house."

We all were belly laughing.

I was doing well, and the week was coming to an end. Kay had to leave, and I appreciated her coming up to help Jacob and me. Jacob took her to the airport and ensured she had everything she needed.

My appointment with the Breast Surgeon went well; however, my Myositis disease was out of remission because I had to be off of my Methotrexate drug because of surgery. I was taking my medications as directed again. It had taken me a few more weeks to recover.

I had appointments the same day with the Medical Oncologist and Radiation Therapy Oncologist. The physicians' team decided, because of my Polymyositis disease and the data outcome with DCIS, to recommend taking Tamoxifen, an anticancer medication, for five years. They also warned me that it would throw me into menopause and hot flashes.

My breast cancer was hormone-driven. I could not take any drugs other than the one they recommended.

I was highly depressed at this point and placed on depression medication again by my Rheumatologist.

Chapter Ten: What Is Happening to My Life?

I was coping with my diagnosis of breast cancer well, but since I was off some of my Myositis medication, I was out of remission. Consequently, I was weak, fatigued, and nauseous from the Tamoxifen.

Fatigue for a Myositis patient is not the same as simply being tired. With Myositis, the fatigue has to wear away gradually as a result of rest and drinking plenty of liquids which fuel the muscle. Myositis causes the good cells in your body to attack the body. I noticed this more so in my lower legs. It caused me to be unsteady on my feet. I would walk into the door, get weak, and have to sit quickly, or sometimes I would just fall to the floor. It was not uncommon to have scars on my legs and knees.

During my Rheumatologist appointment, she recommended that I take a few weeks off from work and that I make an appointment to see her again in two weeks.

I notified my Radiology Manager and informed her that I had a doctor's recommendation to take off work. She said she understood, but quite honestly, I do not think there was a real comprehension of how Myositis disease was affecting my body. Once the immune system is completely thrown off, it takes more time to get back into remission. It wasn't the breast surgery that was causing me to need more time off work.

Please do not get me wrong. My Radiology Director was very kind and caring, but in my heart, I felt there were questions from her and the staff about my health.

I took the recommended time off, and after my follow-up appointment with my Rheumatologist, I attempted to return to work; however, my body was not ready.

I honestly tried.

After speaking with my Rheumatologist, she felt it was best to take FMLA from work to heal and to get my Myositis disease in remission. I was on short/long term disability and eventually my FMLA without pay.

I returned to work and did the best I could, but I could not work part-time as Team Leader, which I understood. So, I was offered a half-time position in Quality Control with a coworker whom I knew did not care for me, nor did I care for her. I can get along with anyone, but just do not do mean things to me intentionally. I did not need the additional stress in my life; so, I gave my resignation to my Radiology Director.

I needed to take care of my health, and that was first and foremost. Jacob and I had talked about it before I actually resigned. He was alright with my decision.

For four years, I enjoyed working at St. Vincent in Indianapolis as a Team Leader and most of the people with whom I worked. Our parents taught us to be able to work with people regardless of what they think of you because you always take "The High Road And Do Not Go To Their Level." I always have done this in my life with people I work with or in my life period.

Confusion

I remember I came home from work that day and told Jacob.

"I submitted my resignation today," I told Jacob.

"I know that is hard for you, but your health comes first."

I was happy he understood.

"I'll start looking for another job," I reassured him.

"Ok," he said. "I'm ok with that."

It was the Christmas holiday, and we had always gone to Jacob's hometown of Alabama and spent a week with his family. He wanted to spend time with his grandchildren, and I was understanding of that.

Because of my constant fatigue, I had never done much for the holidays anyway other than placing a wreath on the door.

Once we arrived at the hotel in Alabama, I rested for the first day, so my body could have the energy it needed to visit with Jacob's family.

Because my son was overseas, I actually enjoyed spending time with the little ones, but it saddened me that Jacob did not wish to share time between his family in Alabama and mine in the Carolinas. I felt it was selfish, but to keep peace in our home, I put up with it.

Christmas morning, we would go over early to watch the grandchildren unwrap their Christmas gifts. I thoroughly enjoyed seeing the joy on their faces. What I could not comprehend was how Jacob would discuss with his daughter-in-law what the children wanted for Christmas with no involvement from me. I was not used to this type of behavior.

I thought, *How does it make sense to leave your wife out of the decisions that supposedly involve OUR grandchildren?*

This was not how my family operated. It was also not how things had worked in my previous marriage. I was taught (and believed) that both adults were involved in family decisions.

Now that Jacob and I were married, he continued not to involve me in the decisions that involved his children.

I did not understand and felt it was disrespectful to me. In my mind, I could see that I was involved in a dysfunctional family atmosphere. However, I kept my mouth closed, still trying my best to be a good wife and compromise.

When we visited his friends, Jacob and I had the best time, and I really enjoyed them to the utmost. They would cook dinner and have whatever you wanted to drink (alcoholic or non-alcoholic beverages). When they had a gathering of their friends, it was fun and entertaining. Jacob's friends made me feel right at home.

By the time it was time to go home, I was ready. Hotel living for a week was not something I was enjoyed.

Once we returned home and settled for the week, Jacob went back to work, and I was on the computer searching for a job. I had dinner ready for him that evening, and we sat down to eat.

"Why did you quit your job and didn't tell me?" Jacob asked.

I was actually speechless when he asked me this question because we sat down and talked about it in depth prior. "I did talk to you about it first," I said.

"No, you did not," Jacob said.

"Jacob, are you losing your mind?" I asked. "You know we discussed this at length. Why are you saying this to me?"

I was so disgusted, confused, and hurt. I got up from the table, went to our bedroom, shut the door, and cried.

I knew something was happening, but I couldn't speak to him anymore about it that night. I remained in our bedroom, left the kitchen just the way it was, had a shower, and went to bed crying.

I prayed, *Lord, help me understand this man I've married.*

I continued to cry and was so upset. I forgot to say goodnight to him.

The next morning, we both greeted each other with, "Good morning." Jacob prepared for work as usual, embraced me with a hug and kiss, and went to the kitchen to make his oatmeal. Sometimes, I did it for him, but other times he'd do it himself. I showered, dressed, went to the computer, and continued to search for a job.

I had become used to sweeping unresolved issues under the rug. I had to think about my health and the impact that stress would have on my remission.

We fell into a routine. I would have dinner ready, and when Jacob arrived home, we'd eat and discuss job opportunities. Jacob suggested I apply for a job with his employer. I did and continued to apply to other places as well.

A few months went by, and I received an email offering employment contingent on me passing a background check. The email included the salary I would be earning as well.

Jacob and I were elated I had gained employment. I was on my way again in a new direction with my life.

A New Job

My employment began on March 31, 2008, in the disbursements department. I was very happy to be working again. I adjusted very well and had great coworkers and management. My work group was small, and I enjoyed my Team Leader as well. Two of us out of our group worked extremely hard to get priority work done when it came in to process for government business.

This job wasn't as gruesome on my body, so going into work was enjoyable. This job did not operate 24/7, so I actually left work on time and rarely had to work overtime.

Now that I was employed by the government, I had inside knowledge of open positions. I noticed a position in Human Resources as an intern, and I applied. That was a dream for me. The requirements for the position included a bachelor's degree and some knowledge of Human Resources, which I had from previous employments. Although there were several candidates applying for the position, I knew I had a favorable chance of being hired if I passed the interview. A few weeks later, I was notified that I had an interview. I immediately told Jacob at lunchtime because we worked at the same government center.

Time seemed to go by slowly while I waited for some news about the job. In the meantime, I continued to work and enjoyed my current job. One day after arriving home from work, I checked my email and found a letter of contingency for the Human Resources Specialist position. The job offered a better salary and an opportunity to advance. Jacob was well pleased at this point.

Jacob continued to be in some sort of denial when it came to work issues. Although he accompanied me to my doctor appointments to see my Rheumatologist, he still didn't think I was sick because I didn't "look sick." He lacked empathy toward me with the Myositis disease. Jacob was in denial about my invisible, incurable Myositis disease. It was very painful for me to know he felt this way.

My Human Resources Specialist job was going extremely well. My coworkers took me under their wings and taught me extremely well. I was really enjoying my job. Jacob's mood shifted back and forth, and he continued to struggle with me paying off all of my credit cards. I didn't understand why. Together, we had more than enough income to support that decision. He had an issue with me paying off my bills, but he continued not to consult me when he gave money to his children. It seemed contradictory to me.

Dysfunction

Time was just speeding by because I was enjoying my job, and Jacob seemed to have gotten over our previous financial issue. Despite our differences, Jacob and I continued to enjoy our outings on the weekend and to attend church. I loved my husband, and although things were strained between his children and me, I did begin to feel more comfortable with his daughter. I treated them cordially, and they did the same for me in front of their father.

There was clear enabling and codependency between Jacob and his children, but Jacob didn't seem to realize it. Perhaps, some of it derived from the fact that he did not raise his older two sons and felt guilty about not having been there.

I loved my son dearly, but I had done my best to raise him to be independent, which is why he felt secure enough to leave the country to work in a warzone.

However, now, he had decided to come back to the USA to work. I was thrilled, so I shared the good news with Jacob.

Jacob gave Abel a great reference, and he was hired by a contractor at the same place where Jacob and I worked. Abel flew in on the weekend and was to report to work the following Monday. The plan was that he would stay with us for about 4-6 months.

Abel's job was going well. He dressed professionally from head to toe each day for work with a nice shirt, a necktie, and slacks. His coworkers didn't dress professionally, but Abel did, as did I. It was what my parents taught me, and it was what I taught Abel. My son was a very responsible young man, and he wanted to be successful in life.

"Abel has to leave," Jacob announced seemingly out of the blue, "because I can't get to my clothes."

Jacob's clothes were in the closet in the bedroom where my son slept.

I was dumbfounded. My son had just arrived from overseas, began a new job, and was successfully adjusting back into society after being in a warzone. Abel had only been living with us for two months. Jacob's son and his girlfriend had lived with us for nearly six months, but nothing was said. Jacob's son's girlfriend was lazy. She did not cook. She stayed in the bedroom, and later, I found out she had been to prison.

I was so upset. I had to gather myself together after what Jacob had just stated to me. I wanted to leave him and never see him again. I went to my bedroom and cried. How was I going to tell my son he had to leave over such a trivial matter? To me, Jacob was really being pure Satan.

I could not call my family in the Carolinas because I knew they would be furious. I wanted to keep the peace. So, I called my son's Godparents instead and told them what Jacob had done. They were extremely upset over his foolishness.

I knew that Jacob was very envious of my son and my relationship with him. Still, I couldn't believe he would do something like this. Jacob had to know I loved my son with all my heart. I had raised him on my own for nine years. Our bond was extremely strong.

It broke my heart to tell Abel he had to leave.

"Don't worry, Mother," my son said to me as I continued to cry. "I can stay with "T." "T" was his Godbrother who lived in Indianapolis and was working at the same place as we all were.

Five months later, his contract was not renewed, and he was jobless. His plans were to go back overseas, but I really did not want him to go.

Crisis

In the meantime, I was still doing well at my new job and was being promoted to the next level. All my experience in HR was simply wonderful, and I enjoyed my coworkers.

What I didn't enjoy were the winter months. I dreaded them because I knew the toll it took on my body. I was sicker, and my fingers burst and bleed. My fingers hurt so badly. It was painful even wearing gloves. My left forearm and the side of my abdomen had red spots spreading everywhere. They were itchy. I made an appointment to go to my Primary Care Physician.

At my appointment, I was diagnosed with shingles. My immune system was weakened. I was given pain medication and Gabapentin. I immediately notified my supervisor to make her aware of the status. I told her that I wasn't sure when I would be returning to work and that I would keep her updated.

The next day, the pain was beginning to be unbearable. The blisters began to appear on my entire left arm, around the left side of my abdomen, and on the left side of my upper back.

I had to call my physician to increase the medication.

I could not stand a sheet to touch my skin. The pain was indescribable, more than extreme and excruciating. I was so drugged up with Gabapentin, 300mg at 4 times per day. The pain medication made me hallucinate.

Jacob spent a week home with me because I could not function or walk to the bathroom. The next week, he had to go back to work, and I was left alone. I was scared to stay in the bedroom because of hearing voices. Jacob would come home at lunchtime to check on me; otherwise, I had to manage on my own. I managed to get to the couch in the sunroom. I remained there until he came home for lunch.

I had to call the physician again about the pain. I had to explain how the shingles looked. I took a photograph and sent it via email to his office. He explained to me that this was the worst case of shingles he had ever seen. Although I was too young to have shingles, my immune system was compromised and since I had chickenpox before, the virus lay dormant until now. It was a rough time, and to this day, I am dealing with peripheral neuropathy on my left side. I do everything my doctor tells me, so I can continue to be mobile and use the left side of my body. All of this is related and intertwines with Polymyositis disease.

I ended going on FMLA until I used my vacation and sick leave. During this period, a neuroma developed in my left toes. Because of extreme pain, I had to walk with a cane. I was going through a crucial time of my life with sickness. My Myositis disease ended up out of remission again because my immune system was too weakened to fight all of what was going on in my body.

I called my Rheumatologist to obtain advice about being out of remission. I had to increase my Prednisone. I was sinking into a deep depression. I was placed on depression medication again. After a visit with my Primary Care Physician, I was referred to an Orthopedic Surgeon for my left foot. The shingles were healing and not infectious any longer. They left so many scars, and I still have light scars on my left forearm presently.

I had surgery on the toes of my left foot in July 2011. I had to get it done because I could not walk without a cane or sometimes a wheelchair if worsened. It was going to take some time to heal because of the Polymyositis disease as well.

During this time period, I had requested telework at home right before surgery. I was completing my work task on time, and there was no problem except with one staff member who was displeased that I was able to telework, and she could not.

Had she been as sick as me? I would have traded positions and let her go through what I had and was continuing to go through.

I was managing to get up with pain while taking pain medication. Sometimes, I was not able to log onto the computer until 9 am because my pain medication made me so drowsy. My Myositis disease was full-blown out of remission with the stress of trying to get well and the stress from my job.

What I did know was the cold weather was quickly declining my health.

I went to the Rheumatologist and explained what was going on. Jacob had to take me; it was too far for me to drive. At times, I could tell he was becoming frustrated and agitated with me also.

My Rheumatologist advised me to relocate to a warmer climate. She wrote a letter, and I submitted it to my supervisor. She forwarded it to the HR Director. Well, to make a long story short, my request was denied by the HR CEO. He stated that I could continue to work from home in Indianapolis.

There was a battle.

If my Rheumatologist stated in her letter that I had to relocate to a warmer climate, what was the real problem? We had other staff in the same HR Department and other departmental wide who were teleworking out of state.

Why couldn't I telework out of state because of my health?

They disrespected me.

"You can relocate to Tampa, Florida," upper management offered.

But they were going to lower my rank and salary.

"No," I said, point blank. "There are other employees teleworking with no health issues. So why am I being punished for having health issues?"

I knew winter weather was approaching again, and my body would not be able to tolerate the cold weather. Jacob and I spoke about it, and he stated I was going home to North Carolina for one month. Then, I would go to Orlando, FL.

There was so much planning to do because we decided we would build our home in Orlando. I went on a Leave of Absence from my employer without pay.

My health was a priority!

I left in November 2011 and headed for North Carolina to live with my sister for one month. I was there for the Thanksgiving Holiday. Jacob was continuing to plan ahead for me to arrive in Orlando.

I enjoyed the month with my sister. Afterward, I drove to Orlando right after Thanksgiving by myself. I was so tired. I had to stop in Savannah, GA and sleep overnight. I knew it was best before I got into a car accident from fatigue. My body was exhausted from the stress of my illness and the stress of being on Leave of Absence.

Jacob was very concerned with me driving down by myself. The car was packed with all my winter clothes and summer clothes.

All I kept repeating to myself was, "God does not place on us no more than we can bear."

Chapter Eleven: Life Changing Events

I arrived safely in Florida the next day with all the information and instructions given by Jacob. I was in a new state. I was extremely exhausted and did not know my way around. I had visited Orlando as a tourist before. I went to the theme parks but nothing to this magnitude. I had reservations in Altamonte Springs, FL. at the Embassy Suites for one week.

Jacob was coming down midweek, so we could relocate to a one-bedroom apartment while our new home was being built.

I had gone online while living with my sister in Greensboro, North Carolina to locate a temporary place to live for six months. I had spoken with the owner, and he sent me photographs in addition to what I had seen online. I had already signed the contract after communicating with Jacob.

He viewed the apartment online and spoke with the owner of the condo as well. Little did I know our new home was on the other side of town - 35 minutes away from the hotel on the northeast side of town. Jacob had booked a midweek flight, and we located the one-bedroom condo in a very nice, quaint area which was gated in Altamonte Springs, FL. Just driving up to it, I knew I would feel safe while Jacob would be traveling back and forth to Indianapolis because he was still working while I had to take a Leave of Absence from work.

As soon as Jacob and I relocated to the condo, we had to make sure I was settled, so he could get back to work. He would be returning in a few weeks. I slept on a single, inflatable queen mattress. At first, we had to sleep on the floor with a regular inflatable mattress. I went and purchased a super queen size mattress, which was thicker because I was having a difficult time getting off the floor. My body was too weak to push myself up from the floor.

The condo was located on the 2nd floor, and this was not helping me at all since my body had weakened to a point. I was just barely getting around. My Polymyositis was out of remission. At this point, I had no Primary Care Physician or Rheumatologist. I had to locate them in Orlando once I settled in the condo. I had all my medications from my physicians before I departed from Indianapolis.

Jacob had a son who lived in Orlando. He worked in the music industry. No one ever knew when he was in town. Jacob had contacted him to ask him to assist me when I needed help if he was available. I had no choice but to call his son to help me finish unpacking the car. Jacob could not lift the heavy luggage filled with clothes as well as other items I had in the car.

His son came over and helped me. I was so grateful. His son was a very nice gentleman and strived to meet his goals in life. Jacob had this son out of wedlock while married to his former wife before marrying me. I always wondered why he never told his former wife the truth. He was such a wonderful son. He had very good manners and was very respectful of me.

I had purchased the inflatable mattress but could not carry it upstairs to my condo. I did not know anyone in my condo building. While going in and out, I noticed a married couple in the condo located under me. I prayed to God that they would help me get the mattress box upstairs.

Well, I knew they could tell me yes or no. I went and knocked on my neighbor's front door. His wife came to the door. I introduced myself. I told her that I was new in town and that I lived above them. I explained to her that I needed assistance with the mattress that needed to be taken to my condo from my car. She immediately told me her husband would not mind assisting me. They had two adorable little boys. She went and got her husband. He came to the door. We introduced ourselves. The mattress was taken upstairs and placed in the bedroom.

"Do you need assistance inflating it," he asked.

"No, I think I got it from here, but thank you so much," I replied.

"Ok, let me know if you need anything else," he offered. "Just come down anytime."

He left, and I locked the door. I unboxed the mattress, but I could not find how to inflate that mattress for anything. I even read the instructions. I just think my mind was too exhausted. I really did not want to go back downstairs to ask him when he had just offered to do it while he was here. I felt like a little fool going back downstairs and knocking on the door AGAIN. His wife came back to the door.

"I'm so sorry," I said, embarrassed. "But would you ask your husband to help me inflate the mattress? He offered, but I thought I would be able to do it on my own."

"No problem," she said with an understanding smile. She went to get her husband.

"I'm so sorry," I said again to him this time. "I can't seem to figure it out."

"No worries," he said with a kind smile. "These things happen."

My neighbors were so very kind. We went into the condo, and he looked at the inflatable mattress. He realized I had not taken the plug out of the mattress. Of course, it wouldn't inflate with the pump while the plug was still intact. I felt like a PURE TEE FOOL! We laughed about it. I thanked him and tried to give him some money, but he refused to accept it.

"That what neighbors do," he said, "help each other in need.

I thanked him again before he left.

I had taken a shower and wasn't feeling well at all. I was feeling like I was coming down with a bad cold. Although it was December, the weather in Florida was very chilly, and I was surprised. I did not know it would be like this. I thought Florida was known for year-round warm weather!

Little did I know that in the months of December through February, it gets really chilly in the mornings. Well before noon, the temperature increases to the high 70s and 80s. Still, I loved the weather and was thankful I had clothes fitting for the early morning chill.

During the night, I noticed that I was getting sicker. My voice was very hoarse, and I was not feeling well at all. I immediately called Jacob to inform him that I was going to find an Emergency Care Center to get something for a cold. I got dressed and was happy I didn't have to travel far. I'd seen a clinic just down the street from our condo. I arrived, registered as a new patient (which takes time), and willed myself to have the endurance for all the forms and questions. Afterward, I asked the receptionist about the wait and was thankful to learn that it would only be 10-15 minutes. Finally, the Medical Assistant called me back.

"I just relocated to Orlando," I explained.

The physician asked me many questions from the history questionnaire.

"I'm out of remission with Polymyositis disease," I told him.

"You have the flu," he said plainly.

It explained why I was weaker than normal and could barely move. I was given medication, advised to go home and rest, and told to locate a Rheumatologist right away. I got my medications filled at the Urgent Care Center which was so convenient. I called Jacob on the way from the Urgent Care Center. He said he was going to get a flight down right away because I could barely drive or go back upstairs to our condo. I finally got to the condo and went straight to lie down on the inflatable mattress. I was literally so sick; I could barely get up to go to the bathroom or try to eat anything.

Jacob's flight arrived the next day in the late evening. I do not even recall how he arrived home to our condo. I was out of it completely. He immediately tried to get me to drink more liquids, broth, and soup to gain some strength.

I was certain all the driving I'd done had weakened my already compromised immune system.

I thought, *What else can happen?*

Jacob and I were building our new home, and I had to find another government job so that I wouldn't lose my status due to my current Leave of Absence.

Looking back, it's a wonder I didn't have a nervous breakdown.

However, I kept praying every single moment for God's invention. I knew, "This Too Shall Pass." I kept my mind on the saying our parents taught us when our faith seemed too weak. I kept my faith strong.

I got better, and before Jacob left to return to Indianapolis, we traveled over to the place where our new home was going to be built. He wanted to teach me how to drive to the northeast side before he headed back to Indianapolis. We went over a couple of times. He let me drive, so I would know how to get there when he departed. He always told me to get back on I-4 interstate and begin again if I got lost.

My directions were to get off I-4 and head 408E. Somedays, I must admit I had to call him a couple of times for the directions because I would get lost. But by the third time, I had learned how to go to our new home site. It would take five months to complete construction.

I was very lonely in this big city of Orlando. Each day I applied for a job, and in between, I checked our homesite. It was a 35-minute drive. Jacob and I would communicate throughout the day because he was concerned about me. He wanted to ensure that the building of our home was going as planned.

It was like I was in another world without anyone I knew at all. I knew I had to get back in church. So, I reached out to my stepson in Orlando.

"You all are welcome to attend the church I attend," he offered. "Or there is another one I can recommend, but it's kind of uppity."

"What do you mean by that," I laughed.

"They dress up and wear big hats every Sunday," he explained. "It's a Black American congregation. The church that I attend is nondenominational, and the attendees are of varying nationalities and ethnicities."

"Thank you," I said. "When your dad returns to town, he and I would like to go with you."

I could tell he was happy about that.

Jacob came into town, and we did attend church with my stepson. I would have loved to refer to him as our son, but Jacob wasn't doing a good job blending his family with me. I was lost for direction in words as to how to greet them.

Should I say stepson or just son?

However, with this particular son, who was the baby boy, I felt comfortable calling him *son*.

We went with our son to the church he was attending on a regular basis. I enjoyed the church service and the pastor; however, it was too contemporary for me. I enjoyed the singing and praise, even though we stood for almost the entire service singing. The pastor could really sing and had CD's available for sale. Our son knew him personally. He delighted in introducing us as his parents to his pastor and even got us autographed CDs of his pastor singing in psalms and preaching.

I enjoyed listening to both when Jacob returned to Indianapolis.

Jacob was still living in our home in Indianapolis while taking care of me in Orlando. I highly commended him for him taking care of the finances. I had saved some funds to assist him.

Time was going by extremely quickly. There were problems with the building of our home. I had to reach out to Jacob daily on the status after his work shift.

I found a Rheumatologist on the side of town where I was currently living, and I really liked him. He had a great bedside manner. He was calm, and he listened carefully. His receptionist and the medical assistant staff was very good and well organized. This was a great feeling for the patient care I was expecting to receive, and I felt very comfortable (Presently, I am still going to the same Rheumatologist for great patient care).

I also located a Primary Care Physician on the side of town where our home would be. It would be a closer drive looking to the future.

My health was gradually going back into remission with the Myositis disease. However, I was still a little stressed because I was continually applying for employment each day but wasn't having any success. I was starting to get depressed. I knew I could not worry too much because that would impact my health, so I decided to visit the "uppity church" our son had mentioned. He told me where it was located.

I went the following Sunday. It was the 11 am church service at Macedonia Missionary Baptist Church, Pastor Willie C Barnes and Lady Anita Barnes. I arrived, was greeted so kindly, and was given a program at the door before entering the sanctuary. I really enjoyed the church service and even stood to be recognized as a guest.

I really enjoyed the old-time religion which I came from. And the choir singing was so touching to my soul. It fulfilled a need within me, and deep inside, I felt this was the place where I was supposed to be.

Each day, I would continue searching for employment and checking on our new homesite. My health was improving somewhat. I kept leaning on my faith, and praying things would get better.

Even still, there were times I was so lonely. In the evening, I would call a few of my family members who were retired back in the Carolinas and my close friends. Jacob would call me throughout the day and also at bedtime.

It was especially tiresome at times when I had to do laundry. The laundromat was in another building. I could not leave my clothes unattended, and since there was nowhere to sit, I was miserable. I managed to wash clothes every two weeks because I had enough clothes with me to prevent weekly washes.

I found out our new home would be completed on time in spite of the few hiccups that had occurred along the way. I was so very happy. Our new home was going to be absolutely beautiful. I loved the floor plan we'd chosen. Jacob and I had made several trips to Orlando before deciding on a location. For a couple of years, we traveled back and forth, looking at different areas. We both knew we wanted to retire to Orlando; however, we had no idea it would come so soon.

Christmas came, and due to all that had happened in the past few months, this day was no different than any other day. I was thankful and grateful to God for being alive each day I had awoken. We enjoyed the holiday as usual, the best we could. In the rental condo where we were staying, I did not do any decorations for Christmas because of my lack of energy. I had to reserve as much as possible to do the day to day things I needed to get done. I had been diagnosed with Myositis since 1995, and by now, I knew the little quirks that affected my body. I knew what I needed to do to remain in remission.

I was beginning to get frustrated. We would be moving into our new home soon (April 24, 2012), and I still hadn't found a job. I knew I had to find employment. Believe me; it wasn't because I wasn't searching every day online. When Jacob arrived in town for a week, we went to a government building to the Human Resources Department. I was dressed appropriately and armed with my resume in my hand. We located HR and went up to the second floor.

Somehow, Jacob managed to get past security in the main entry. We went to the second floor and straight into the HR office. The receptionist was sitting at the desk.

Jacob asked if the HR Director was in for the day. She was, and we were able to speak with her. Jacob accompanied me into her office. She and I exchanged pleasant conversation about my experience, and I informed her I had applied on the website several times.

She explained that they were short-staffed, so the process took longer. She told me that if my application were selected, it would be sent to the hiring manager, who would set up an interview. She also explained that preferences were given to individuals who were veterans or applicants with disabilities.

Weeks went by, and no notification was sent from them. I kept praying and continued my daily routine of checking on our new home and keeping Jacob updated on things in Florida.

Our new home was finally ready, and it was simply gorgeous, our dream home in Orlando, FL. We had a walk-thru scheduled a few days from closing on April 24th. In between this time, I was notified that I had received the contingency for the Human Resources Specialist job as long as my background check was great. Plus, I was only getting a transfer from the other government facility since I was on Leave of Absence. This was great news for Jacob and me.

We closed on our home on time and immediately returned to Indianapolis to prepare for the relocation of all our furniture from the condo we owned in Indianapolis. We immediately relocated because I had to report for duty two weeks later. It was an extremely stressful time.

We had North American to load and move us. Once the furniture arrived, they unloaded and placed all the furniture in the appropriate rooms as well as the labeled boxes.

Jacob was still working in Indianapolis; however, he had taken some time off from work to get both of us somewhat settled in our new home. Our dream home was valued at over half a million dollars. Jacob had also chosen the best lot with a lake view.

I loved this two-story home and the fact that our master suite was located on the first floor. Jacob had the family room extended along with a pool and enclosure. We had a total of 4 bedrooms, 3 full bathrooms, and 1 ½ bath leading from inside the home to the pool area. There were sliding glass doors in our master suite, which led to the pool area, as well as the family room. The house had a beautiful full kitchen with a huge island, a bar area, and a kitchen nook. Upstairs was another master suite with a full bathroom. There was also a bonus room entertainment area along with Jack and Jill bedrooms and a full bathroom shared between the rooms. The house had a two-car garage and a single car garage on the opposite side of the house, which was for the office. There was a doorway entry from the office on the outside to prevent people from coming through our home for business matters.

Our entire home was decorated very nicely; however, it had taken about a year to get all items completed at our home. Jacob was very impatient on the decorating part because boxes sat in the living room for a while. He grew frustrated over nothing. I told him he could remove them if he wished them to be removed faster.

I had just begun to work, and he was trying to begin teleworking from home from Indianapolis. He had placed our condo in Indianapolis for sale. I continued working. I enjoyed my job; however, it was nothing like my last employer. This government center did not have the funds to purchase the necessary items to help us do our jobs because their budget was limited. I did the best I could at my job; although, it was very stressful.

Our team was small, which meant we had to work diligently. Still, I came in with the same grade despite my past employer's unfair recommendation. I felt that they had tried to discriminate against me. Even now, there is always the "Good Boy" network to contend with.

I enjoyed my job as well as the people with whom I worked. This made my job more meaningful.

Our duties included hiring physicians for hospitals and clinics. I had to attend meetings with the CEO of the hospital to give updates on the physicians' hiring status and in what part of the hiring process we were. I felt that we were working on an assembly line because those physicians were already needed. Once we hired them, some didn't stay long due to patient load and low salary even though they were given generous bonuses.

Jacob and I were enjoying life, and all seemed to be going well. He decided to retire in December 2012 because he was quite dissatisfied with the way I was treated and the way his job went down. However, it occurred, to this day, I still do not know why he was changed from Directorate of Military Pay to Call Center Director. He never wanted to discuss it. He did not even go back for a retirement party in Indianapolis. Whatever it was, he still felt mistreated, and I did as well in regard to the teleworking and the denial.

Jacob and I had talked about me retiring from the government center. I really wanted to volunteer overseas; however, after speaking with all my Physicians (Specialists), it was not a good idea because of my overall health. I retired in May 2013 from the government employer in Orlando. I was eligible for early retirement from Cape Fear Valley Medical Center. Jacob and I had fully discussed this before I had given my resignation because he knew exactly how much I had in retirement from CFVMC, and he was alright with it. I was saddened to leave, but it was best for my health.

Our life was going well, and we were meeting new friends. Jacob began to attend Macedonia Missionary Baptist Church with me. I told him I enjoyed the pastor's delivery of the Word of God. Jacob went a few times and felt we needed to visit a few other churches. I knew in my heart that this was the church for me.

Once Jacob continued to go a few more times, he introduced himself to the pastor as the pastor shook hands with members and visitors as they left service on Sunday mornings. Jacob discovered Pastor Barnes was from Alabama as well. He was really into attending church now because Jacob's hometown state was Alabama.

Life was going well for both of us. However, Jacob had mentioned on occasion that I had quit my jobs, and I would just look at him in awe because we had fully discussed things before I left my jobs. I was beginning to think Jacob was getting early dementia. He did not recall any of our conversations.

After I retired, I wanted to do something more meaningful in life, so I spoke with Jacob about launching a 501(c)(3) nonprofit organization. He was fine with my decision and even gave me funds to help launch it in April 2016.

The launch was very successful.

Although countless hours went into this launch, no one, including the Board of Directors, would be paid.

Jacob had been having chest pains on and off. He finally made an appointment to go and see the Cardiologist, where we both were seen as patients. I had problems with my blood pressure fluctuating. It began back in Indianapolis and continued until I arrived in Orlando and thereafter.

Jacob had a cardiac catheterization scheduled. It determined that he had blocked arteries, although he had already had stents.

I was always concerned about his health more so than he was with my own illness because, in his words, "I Did Not Look Sick."

This perception made me upset and angry because I had Myositis disease, and no one would understand what that meant but a "Myositis Warrior." It was painful to me for friends to think I was not sick and believe me; I knew they did not.

At some point, I had to let all those perceptions leave my mind completely to remain at peace with myself, and I knew one man knew it all "Jesus Christ." Once I "**let go and let God**," my worries about other persons' perceptions of me did not matter. That is why I am bold enough to be an Advocate for Myositis and Breast Cancer patients, survivors, and those persons who have lost their battle to these diseases.

Jacob's results from the Cardiologist were not good.

"Your husband is going to need surgery," the Cardiologist explained to me with compassion and care in the hospital lobby.

I began to weep.

"Don't worry," he said and placed his hand on my shoulder, "I'll take great care of him."

I knew he would. He is one of the best cardiologists I have encountered because of his patient care and concern for his staff.

Jacob understood the seriousness of his diagnosis, and he was immediately referred to a Cardiac Surgeon. Once we met this surgeon, we knew he was the one God sent for a great outcome for Jacob's surgery.

He came into the room for our first appointment, introduced himself, and gave each one of us an embrace just like he was a person we had already known. He made us feel better about everything that was going to take place from preop to postop. He had the greatest team of staff working for him, from the receptionist to the preop surgery schedulers. It was a very organized one-stop-shop.

Everyone was so compassionate and caring, something I wish my husband showed towards me when I was not feeling well. Jacob would brush my concerns aside.

I was determined to uphold my vows when it came to caring for my husband. I knew I had a Myositis disease that made my body muscles weak, but I was going to do my best to ensure he healed properly after his upcoming heart surgery.

Jacob's surgery was scheduled for August 2016.

He had a large support system that included his children and close friends (both in Orlando and from Indianapolis), his younger brother and wife, who lived in Florida, and his other brother and wife, who were from Alabama. My son was coming too.

Chapter Twelve: Accepting What I Cannot Change

A Change of Heart

The night before Jacob's heart bypass surgery, he decided he wanted to have a cookout with family and friends. In my mind, I thought, *Who does this?* I even said, "Jacob, do you realize you are having major surgery, and we have to be at the hospital at 5 am?"

He dismissed me like he always had. In his mind, I was telling him what to do, which was frequently what he said to me. He didn't understand that I was only trying to look out for his wellbeing. Jacob had no empathy, not even for himself.

As a matter of fact, he did not even go to the Cardiologist when he first began having chest pains until the pains became constant. He would look tired and drained. At the time, I was convinced it was all from playing golf in the hot sun. Most days, he would come home, lie on the couch, and fall asleep. I would not disturb him.

I could see Jacob was changing towards me before we left Indianapolis. He talked about me to his best friend. He says he needed an outlet; however, in my opinion, the best outlet would have been God and a therapist (which he did not believe in going to). Jacob felt he knew everything and did not wish to hear criticism from anyone or advice on things he needed to change in his life.

Once I had married Jacob, I could definitely see that in him. I assumed it was the ego part of him that was cultured from being a retired CSM. Whatever the cause, I knew my husband needed mental health sessions as well as his family.

Some of Jacob's family and friends agreed with me and tried to talk him out of having that gathering of people at our home that evening. Still, he would not listen, not even to his best friend.

"Jacob, you need to cut this evening short and get some rest for your surgery," Jarrett said.

"I'm ok," he replied.

I could tell that Jarrett was frustrated. I was frustrated with him too, and decided to walk away from the conversation. I knew if he didn't listen to this best friend, he would not listen to me.

Not much later, Jarrett and his wife left to go back to their hotel room.

What could I say if he wouldn't listen to his best friend whom he had known since the beginning of his military career?

Jacob was a man who knew everything. You could not tell him anything, even if it was in a caring and thoughtful manner. Again, I believe his military career played a huge role in his behavior. I also feel he suffered from Post-Traumatic Disorder and a passive-aggressive personality. Today, he would still deny that he needs mental health assistance.

Things Work Out

My son had called me to let me know his flight had arrived. I told Jacob I was leaving to pick him up from the airport. When I returned home, it was late that evening, around 10:30 or 11:00 pm.

Jacob was sitting on the lanai, still talking to his children. I called him into the house to discuss the sleeping arrangements.

"My children are sleeping here at the house," Jacob said flatly.

He had not given any thought to my son and where he would sleep. At this point, I was extremely upset. My son had worked all day and still flew down because he cared enough to be there through Jacob's surgery.

Unfortunately, this wasn't unusual behavior. Jacob was very selfish and had never discussed one thing with me when it came to *his* children. I had no say so in anything, and this was how it would be throughout our entire marriage.

I was furious and decided to take my son to find him a hotel. We went out that night, and I had forgotten it was the beginning of the fall semester at the universities in Orlando. All the hotels were booked up. My son and I sat in my car, calling hotels on our cellular phones, trying to locate a hotel that was nearby. It was already close to midnight, and Jacob had to be at the hospital at 5 am.

I was angry, frustrated, and quite fatigued. The stress of dealing with Jacob and entertaining family and friends who had come into town because of his surgery was accumulating.

My son had been driving because he knew I was not only fatigued but frustrated with Jacob and his poor decisions. We decided to park.

My son always seemed to know what to say.

"Mother, it's going to work out for the good; please do not get too upset," he said, "Think of *your* health."

I paused, gathered my thoughts, and began to focus and view things more logically. I recalled the hospital telling Jacob and me that if we needed a place for our immediate family, there was a hotel especially designated for family that wasn't even a block away from the hospital. I called them, and they had a few rooms available specifically for these situations. I was so thankful to God that night. I began to cry because literally I did not think we would find a place for my son to stay.

"And we know all things work together for good to them that love God." Romans 8:28 KJV

Once my son was settled, I went back home. I could tell he was quite worried about me. I told him to rest. I said that I would text him once I arrived back home safely. When I arrived home, Jacob was still up talking to one of his sons.

When it came to his children, Jacob had always been very disrespectful towards me. In my heart, I knew it was because he felt extremely guilty over his lack of involvement in their lives when they were children. His daughter was the only one of his children whom he raised from birth until she left for college.

I texted my son to let him know that I made it safely. Then, I showered and went to bed. I left Jacob up. He knew I was upset but didn't seem to care. But thankfully, God cares.

The Right Thing to Do

Jacob and I arrived at the hospital on time at 5 am. I was already fatigued, but I knew I had to remain with him throughout his surgery and his entire recovery period. I had no idea what he had discussed with his children because I was not involved in their conversations at all.

It is standard protocol for the hospital staff only to communicate with the spouse or whoever had the healthcare power of attorney.

I was there when Jacob went back for surgery. I embraced and kissed him to let him know he was going to be fine. Although our home situation was not at its best, I truly loved him even though he was not strong enough to stand up for me with his children and to respect me as his wife.

Jacob's best friends and his brother-in-law were waiting thereafter in the waiting room, along with Sue, my girlfriend from Orlando, and Abel. We greeted each other with an embrace of love and sat talking quietly.

Other members of Jacob's extended family came up as well. A very nice couple I had met a few times whom I had shared a few cordial conversations with were there. They had even spent a weekend with us before in our home. They were from Florida, about 2 hours or more away. I thanked them for coming as well.

I kept waiting for Jacob's children to arrive, so I texted his oldest son. Unbeknownst to me, Jacob had told them not to come to the hospital until that afternoon of his surgery.

Here we all sat in the hospital waiting room while Jacob's children were back at our home still lying in bed sleeping or whatever they decided to do for the day. They were going by what their father had stated for them to do instead of caring enough to be there for me as their stepmother. I felt his children should have known better because they were adults, and this was their father having surgery this morning.

There was so much on my mind. Worrying was not the thing to do. I forced myself to focus on what I could control. I just prayed to God at this moment because getting upset was not the right thing to do.

I was really concerned about how the surgery was going. I knew Jacob's heart was not in the best condition because he had already had several stents placed. I was updated by the waiting room personnel when I requested because it was taking longer than normal.

I felt that Jacob should not have had that cookout the previous night because he may not do well with general anesthesia. Hours and hours went by, and the surgery continued. I kept family and friends updated as soon as I was told anything about Jacob's surgery status.

Finally, the Cardiac Surgeon came out to speak with me, and we went to a corner of the room for privacy.

"There is some good news and some not so good news," he stated.

He told me he did all the arteries he could do while Jacob was under anesthesia; however, due to the amount of damage and the extended time Jacob was under anesthesia, he felt it was too risky to attempt the other blockage.

"If he has to have surgery in the future, it would be open heart surgery again."

Jacob was a blessed man, and I was a blessed wife. I was grateful.

Because of the cookout the night before, Jacob was tired, so it took more time for him to be aroused from the anesthesia. This was a grave concern for the nurses and the surgeon.

Hours passed before I was allowed to go back to see my husband.

I was not called back to see Jacob for hours. I gave an update to family and friends in the lobby. And per Jacob's instruction, I texted the oldest son the update.

Clearly, we were not a blended family. I felt that I tried, but it was something Jacob didn't want. Moreover, a few of his children did not want anything to do with me.

It hurt, but my parents taught us to "feed them out of a long handle spoon and still love them from a distance." That is how I survived the lack of communication and disrespect. It was quite a dysfunctional family, and I found myself in the middle of it. I had not grown up this way. While no family is perfect, my family is close and loving.

We can agree to disagree and still love one another. It's the right thing to do.

Keeping the Peace

If I recall, Jacob's children arrived at the waiting room later that afternoon with a nonchalant attitude. My girlfriend noticed right away. I was thankful I was not the only one to notice.

Before Jacob could accept anyone back to see him, two of his family members had to leave because of knee problems. They had been sitting for a long period of time. I felt Jacob's family was a little agitated because I was the only one who could go back to see him. They should have understood I was the spouse, and at this time, Jacob was not doing too well coming out of the anesthesia. He was struggling.

Earlier, when I went to see him, he did not look well at all. I was somewhat teary-eyed; however, I had to be calm and not let him see me cry. He probably would not have known anyway since he was still not awake enough to know I was there. I rubbed his hand, which seemed to be the only part of his body that wasn't attached to something.

Finally, after some time, family and friends could go back to see Jacob. I knew it would be difficult for his children to see him, especially his daughter. She was crying, and I embraced her. I knew it was painful to see their father that way. It was difficult for me too, as his wife, but I knew I had to be strong.

Later that evening, Jacob had progressed well. Everyone had left, including his children, who went back to our home. I stayed and was exhausted mentally and physically with all that had gone on the night before and all that was going on today.

Jacob was in the Intensive Care Unit for three nights. My son stayed at the hospital with me the entire time, but Jacob's children didn't. For three nights, he and I slept in recliners. He slept some; then, I would. My son paid for a hotel just to place his clothes because he never left my side.

"Mother, you go to sleep. I will take over tonight and go back to see Mr. Jacob when the nurse comes out to get you. I will go back to check on him instead."

The recliners were hard, and I was so cold. That was the Myositis disease. I asked the nurses for extra blankets.

In my mind, I thought Jacob would have planned for his children and me to rotate our schedules and take turns sitting with him. This would have allowed me to go home and get rest. But that did not happen at all.

Once again, there was no communication or decision making with his wife.

When his children were not at the hospital with me, they were at our home enjoying sleeping in and swimming in our pool. I guess they thought they were on vacation instead of assisting with their father's medical care.

I was confused, but it wasn't anything new. This lack of concern had been happening throughout our entire marriage. To an extent, I had grown immune to it. My goal was just to keep the peace and to do my best to uphold my wedding vows.

Grace and Mercy

My son and I were at McDonald's, getting something to eat when my cell phone rang. It was the hospital.

"Mrs. Gordon, your husband was in the process of being moved to a step-down cardiac unit when he developed problems."

We rushed back to the hospital, and on our way, I called Jacob's oldest son to make him aware of the situation. We arrived, found out where Jacob was and went there immediately. They explained what had happened.

When I went into Jacob's room, his brother was already there sitting with him. Evidently, while I was out, the nursing staff had gone out to the waiting room and asked if anyone was there for Jacob. Since he was there, he had been allowed to go back immediately.

I asked Jacob how he was feeling, and he said he was feeling much better. However, his blood pressure had fluctuated quite a bit, so the nurses told us it was best to take him back to the ICU.

I went out to speak with the nurse, and she gave me a new code to use for the immediate family. He was not supposed to have too many visitors at this point. Well, before I knew it, there was a lot of discussion coming from one particular son.

He wanted to know why the password was changed and why they did not have it when they arrived. It was a hot mess, I must say. Had they been there for the care of their father, the attitude I had gotten could have been prevented. I had *just* received the passcode and hadn't had time to give it to them. They also wondered how the uncle got in to see their father before them. That was a no brainer situation. Again, I say had they been there for their father the entire time as well as giving me some support, all of that would have been prevented.

A few of them really thought I had done this intentionally.

I just had to pray my way through the dysfunction going on around me. I asked God to cover me with His grace and mercy.

Even with all of their fuss, Jacob's children returned to our home while my son and I remained with Jacob for his entire hospital stay. I was literally exhausted.

Jacob had progressed well, and it was time for him to go home. Sue had a recliner that we could use; however, I had to rent a truck from U-Haul to move the recliner from my girlfriend's home to our home. By phone, I located a place close to our home and not far from my girlfriend's home. Jacob's younger son and my son were waiting at the U-Haul rental to help. I paid for the truck, and they rode in it to follow me to my girlfriend's home to pick up the recliner.

As I was driving down 408E, I just fell asleep. I was in the middle lane drifting to my right, and the car horns were blowing like crazy. I woke up and realized at that moment how exhausted I was without a comfortable night sleep in a bed for three nights and four days. It was only God that kept me from causing a multi-car accident on that day. I heard of people falling asleep at the wheel of their cars; however, I did not think it could happen to me. Believe me, it happened. Riding alone with no music playing in the car, I just fell asleep. That is exactly how easy it is for someone to fall asleep at the hands of their steering wheel without them realizing it happened.

Lord, Give Me Strength

Jacob was discharged from the hospital, and the recliner was there at our home. The necessary items he needed were at home. Our home was well prepared for his arrival, so he may begin the healing process.

Other family and friends had departed. Jacob's daughter stayed with us for a week, and I was so grateful. His daughter was a great assistance. She cooked dinner and tidied up the house.

When she left, it was just Jacob and me. He had multiple incisions from this chest area to his leg and arms. I had to use entirely white towels when showering with him. I had a chair right beside the shower door. As we carefully came out of the shower, I was just as wet as he was;

however, I ensured he was safely in place, sitting firmly in the chair.

I washed 15 white towels every single day, prepared his meals, and drove him to every appointment for 6 weeks. I also took him out riding around, so he would not go stair crazy because he was an outdoors person, especially when it came to playing golf.

I would be so fatigued; however, I knew I could take care of him by the grace of God.

I would not sleep at night in a deep REM of sleep; I needed to hear him call me if needed. He would call me and tell me he had to use the restroom. He did not wish to use the urinal because difficulty urinating. He stated to me, "I am not going to use that side chair toilet." I knew this was not the right time to get him upset nor myself. I would go to his side of the bed, swing his legs off a little, and get in the correct position to lift him up. We would count to three, and on the three, he would be rising up into a sitting position.

With my Myositis disease, I wasn't supposed to be lifting him this way. We called the insurance company to get a nurse to come to the house. He also needed physical therapy. When the nurse came, I thought she was coming to help bathe him or to assist me during the hours we needed her the most. That was not the case at all. She was a Registered Nurse and just took notes on the status of how he was doing. She recorded blood pressure checks, took his temperature, and checked his heart rate. I was trained in this field to have these skills.

I let her come anyway because during her time with him, I would lie down and rest my extremely fatigued body. I was struggling each day with fatigue, and my energy level was almost nonexistent. However, I kept praying and praying for God to continue to give me the strength to be the best wife while my husband needed me the most. I recalled the wedding vows Jacob and I had taken in front of God as well as having marriage counseling with the chaplain.

Jacob would try to walk outside without me knowing he was out the door. This upset me because I would be yelling his name in the house. "Jacob, where are you?"

He said, "I felt like I could walk outside alone." I called the office. His surgeon stated that as long as he walked to the edge of the driveway, he would be fine with his cane in hand. So, I let him go freely to do his walk when he felt up to it; however, I spent the time peeking out the window to ensure he was steady on his feet.

Doing Physical Therapy at home was great for him and me. It prevented me from getting him up so early and preparing to take him to those appointments 2-3 times per week.

I never gave Jacob his backtalk or expressed to him, "You not sick," like he would tell me sometimes. I know how I felt before he had the surgery. While in Indianapolis or upon relocating to Orlando, I recalled my parents telling us always to be nice to people who treat us badly or talk about us because none of us on this earth are flawless, only God. This dwelled in my heart every single day, even when I know people misjudge me or have something to say. It does not bother me anymore because as Michelle Obama stated, "When they go low, we go high." I must say she knew exactly what she stated was, and I am sure she was persecuted many times.

Jacob recovered quite well and was released as scheduled from his Cardiac Surgeon. His birthday was approaching in November that same year. I wanted to give him a birthday celebration just with our immediate family, his children, my son and his Goddaughters. I planned the entire affair and made sure all the children were included in a group text. The celebration event was for his birthday and successfully recovering from heart surgery. It simply was a beautiful affair; although, I was so extremely fatigued. My body had not recovered when he was sick and not able to get around. I had to pull on him with his weight leaning on my body. He was too proud to be pushed in a wheelchair. Some days I wanted to scream during his recovery time because my little body frame was fragile at this time.

Tough Love

Jacob's celebration was held at an expensive resort. I think Jacob tried to be the "hero" of his family; however, what he failed to see was just giving his children unconditional love was all they needed. He would get items for his birthday, and in one instance, a member of his family was not able to contribute anything. This was the same family that he enabled our entire marriage. Jacob would tell me, "I have the funds, and we have a great life. So why shouldn't I help them if I see they are trying?"

Well, first of all, people need to be able to help themselves. This son couldn't keep a job. The reason he could not keep a job was because of his high temper. Jacob would tell me; he got this personality feature from his mother. Well, he needed a mental health therapist to assist him in dealing with what issues he had and with his well-being. It just seemed that his son could not get his life together, and they had children at home with them. From the time I met Jacob, he was assisting this same son over and over again, and this was not normal. I even told Jacob to stop enabling his family to do the same thing over and over.

He never expressed tough love to his children. Jacob wanted to be their friend. There is a fine line you do not cross with your children. Believe me; you could ask my only child, a son whom I loved dearly. I let him make mistakes, but I also showed him real tough love as being a Single Parent with him. I had to in order for him to be independent in life and have a very successful career.

Most of Jacob's children are very intelligent and smart, but there are responsibility issues with at least one of his sons. He refuses to take responsibility for himself or his family. Jacob brought this same son and his family four cars and two for his grandson. By this account, I would say Jacob has done more than enough. His children are grown and should instead be caring for him. At the time of this writing, he is nearing 71-years-old.

After Jacob's heart surgery, he seemed to want to be on the run from home every single day. He said he was playing golf twice a week, going to the Senior Center to play cards, and on the other days, I could not tell you what Jacob was doing. I trusted him to do the right thing.

However, when your husband does not want to be at home and is gone all day, you begin to wonder what is really going on. He would pack a lunch when he went to play cards and never came home until after 3-4 pm daily. This was not a normal marriage. I would be at home resting once I was on the computer for a few hours. He even quit my nonprofit organization as Vice-President. That came to me a big surprise when he helped me to launch it.

Jacob began to drastically change in 2017. He went on more *Guy Trips,* which was different for me because I was used to it being him and me doing so many things.

I asked him one day, "Jacob, do you have resentment against me because I left my jobs?"

He got quiet and I knew that this was some of the problem. I could read him like a book.

He said one of his friends suggested that he stop taking me on luxury vacations and giving me whatever I wanted.

That made me angry. His friends didn't live with us, nor did they contribute to our household.

He then suggested that I could get a little job.

This really made me angry because I am sure that comment also came at the suggestion of his friends. It was clear that instead of venting to me, Jacob was venting to his friends and maybe even his family.

I was sure Jacob didn't tell his friends that some of the strain on our budget came from him continuing to enable his son, who was always in need. I had retirement income coming in each month, but again, I'm sure Jacob didn't disclose that to his meddling friends either.

I knew that several of his friends did not think I was sick. If only they could trade places with me just for one day, they would be more understanding of what I went through every single day of my life.

You can't judge a person by what you see, and you can't pretend to know what goes on inside a marriage. The people who know what goes on behind closed doors are the people who live there and Jesus.

Missing in Action

While we lived in Orlando, Florida, Jacob left me home alone nine times to travel for guy trips, weddings, trips with his sons, and other mini vacations. But the straw that broke the camel's back was when he left me on a Nebulizer breathing machine (every four hours), a Symbicort inhaler, and a ProAir inhaler.

I felt like he was punishing me because I could not work due to the Myositis disease. I didn't think this was fair since I made sure to disclose my medical history with him fully before we married.

One weekend while Jacob was gone, my oldest Sister Lillie and my niece Tonie were in Daytona Beach, Florida attending their Goddaughter's birthday party. Angel was a very smart, intelligent, and beautiful young lady. I had previously met her and her mom, Carrie, at a Christmas family gathering in Greensboro, North Carolina. They were both so charming. They felt like family members.

Lillie called me on their way back home.

"What's wrong, Miyoshi?" My sister knew me very well.

"Nothing," I replied, attempting to be cheerful. But in my heart, I was so sick.

Not much later, the doorbell rang.

I was wondering who it could be. I wasn't expecting anyone, and if it were someone outside the gate, they would have had to call my phone to gain entry through the gates to our subdivision.

I peeped through the peephole of the door and saw my sister and niece standing there. I immediately opened the door.

"Sis, are you sick? You look very pale." My sister was very concerned.

"I am sick," I admitted.

"Where is Jacob?" She asked. I could see the anger rising up in her face.

"He went to a wedding in another part of Florida," I told her. "We were both invited, but I was too sick to go, and he would not say home with me."

"Dial his number," she insisted, "and hand me the phone."

She and Jacob exchanged words. My sister was not very happy with him. She reminded him that his place was home with his sick wife.

He still didn't come home right away.

Earlier, I had called Jacob's son to ask him if he would bring me something to eat. He did and was very kind about it. It was only God that allowed him to be in town that weekend because he traveled quite a bit for his music. He worked with some of the greatest producers. I had been to his studio before and experienced how they produce the sound for the recording artists.

Jacob came in the next morning, not knowing that my sister and niece were still there. It was earlier than normal. Usually, it was around hotel checkout time when he would return home.

Before leaving, my niece cleaned the bathrooms and made the beds, so I wouldn't have to do it later. My sister asked if I was ok; then, they left. They were both extremely angry with Jacob for leaving me sick, especially when they learned it wasn't the first time and that it happened frequently.

Jacob lived and behaved like he was a single man. I don't know what happened to the man I married. That man was missing in action, and our marriage was going downhill.

Emotionally Abandoned

My marriage was continuing to crumble in front of my eyes. I suggested that we go to an experienced marriage therapist. We did in 2017, but Jacob's heart wasn't in it. He only attended three sessions with me and a few on his own. I could tell Jacob had emotionally left the marriage because he did not wish to speak with our church pastor about our marriage issues. I had to focus on my sanity, so I continued mental health therapy on my own. I knew I needed to practice self-love myself.

Maintaining my sanity was hard because I was living a life I had never lived before. There was so much dysfunction and disrespect.

It was close to Valentine's Day, and Jacob was planning a guy's trip with one of his sons and some friends. They were all married as well. One of the men thought better of the trip and decided, before Valentine's Day, to go home to his wife from the end of the guy's trip. But Jacob didn't.

Instead of staying home with me, he chose to go to Alabama.

Even now, I still don't understand why all of the emotional abuse happened. I did not deserve any of it. I was a great wife to Jacob.

Because I was treated so poorly at home during the entire year, when the Christmas holiday came around, I wished to be with my family in

North Carolina. This was much more favorable than being home alone at Christmas.

Jacob had only been to North Carolina with me for Christmas two or three times during our marriage. We usually spent the holiday with his family. I understood he wanted to be with his grandchildren, but not seeing my family wasn't fair to me.

Jacob was not only unfair to me, but he was also unfair to his children and grandchildren. He had his favorites, and it was evident. It was also evident that we were having trouble in our marriage. I was sure his children knew.

The dysfunction was insane, so I continued my therapy sessions for two years. I was determined to be whole in mind, body, and soul. I wanted to feel like my authentic self again.

With all that I was going through, I prayed continuously throughout the day. I would be sitting in the office looking out the window, wondering where the wonderful, caring man was whom I had married and intended to be married to for the rest of my life.

I really had to give it all over to God because I was literally getting sick in my body. By now, I was taking over 13 pills a day trying to cope.

When I finally told my physicians what was going on in my personal life, they suggested I bring Jacob with me to my next appointment, so he could hear what they were telling me. It would give him the chance to ask questions and to try to have a better understanding of a Myositis disease.

However, I felt Jacob did know, but he wanted a *trophy wife* with a *high income*. Jacob had gotten caught up in the lives of best friends. He frequently spoke about how extremely well they were doing, but we were too.

But Jacob did not see it that way. He seemed to base his opinion on my good days.

If there was a rare day that I didn't feel pain or fatigue, I would ride out to the shopping outlet to get out of the house and to find deals on things I could use as fundraisers for my nonprofit organization. I never knew when these times would come, so I tried to make use of them when I could. But the consequences were punishment with emotional abuse.

"You are not too sick to go to Michael Kors or to host events," Jacob would say in an ugly tone, and it felt like he speared a knife through my heart. I knew that I was trying so hard. I would sometimes lie in bed and cry.

It was painful for me to know that the man I married, loved, and had cared for during his surgery, for whom I had given up time with my family during holidays to spend it with him, and his family would treat me this way.

I realized that Jacob was a very angry man inside. He needed God to intervene in his life. Satan had stolen his soul, and I knew this without a doubt.

I knew that the emotional abuse would stop one day when God intervened and that it would be in His timing, not mine.

In My Right Mind

My left rotator cuff was partially torn from lifting Jacob when he had heart surgery. My body was too fatigued, and my muscles were simply not strong enough. In April 2017, I was in pain and was going to Physical Therapy. The Orthopedic Surgeon did not wish to operate because of the Myositis disease and recommended Physical Therapy instead. PT was assisting me, but I just couldn't lift heavy objects. I continued PT for a two-year period.

I attended a banquet in North Carolina and fell.

There wasn't enough lighting in the restaurant. The lights were dim, and there were no lights along the staircase. Even though I was holding on to the rail as I was going down, I stumbled on the last step and fell.

I tried to catch myself as Jacob was at my side. I saw myself sliding headfirst into the wall. I immediately reached out with my left arm (the one with the partial rotator cuff tear from lifting Jacob). I think I passed out for a second. All I remember was people trying to sit me in a chair.

My left wrist felt as if it was broken and was rapidly turning blue. My left knee was hurting too.

The restaurant manager and staff were very kind. The manager immediately gave Jacob his card just in case I had to go to the hospital. The valet brought our car around, and as we were heading back to the hotel, I told Jacob that I needed to go to the Emergency Room because I was in extreme pain. When we arrived at the hotel, Jacob went inside the hotel to ask where the nearest hospital was. Thankfully it was only about 10 minutes away. We arrived and went inside. I had to wait a long time and decided to lie down on the chairs that were out front.

Finally, after hours of waiting, they called me back.

That's when I heard someone screaming at the top of their lungs. I assumed right away he was on some type of substance and had overdosed.

In the meantime, Jacob kept questioning the staff about how long it was taking for them to see me. He reminded them of how much pain I was in.

Apparently, they were short-staffed, and there was only one ER Physician. When he finally came to where I was, he apologized. Why was it taking so long for me to get care? I was in extreme pain from the fall. I told him for a hospital of this size, with a large patient load, their staffing was unacceptable. He agreed without any hesitation and told me that the hospital was in the process of a merger with another hospital. They hoped things would be better.

I also found out that their Radiology Department was not in the ER, nor was there a Radiologist. Their x-ray system was not digital. They were not even close to a modernized high technology facility.

My sisters and niece came from Greensboro, North Carolina, to make sure I was alright, but I was not. I did the best I could while they visited our hotel room. Jacob went out to get us something to eat; however, he felt uncomfortable with my oldest sister and niece, who had earlier found me sick and him not home.

The next few days, I rested; then, we headed home to Orlando and arrived safely.

I had to make appointments to see my Primary Care Physician and was referred to an Orthopedic Surgeon. I continued my Physical Therapy and also knew I was going to be scheduled for surgery for a now completely torn rotator cuff. My surgery was scheduled for May 7th.

In between having this surgery, Jacob wanted to go to Alabama for Easter Holiday. I went along with him, and once I arrived, Jacob had planned for his grandson to return home with us.

I was in dismay because Jacob had not bothered to discuss this with me. But this was no different than any of the other times he had made decisions without consulting me – this was especially true when it came to his children and grandchildren.

Times like this only made me miss my family more – especially my son, who was overseas. I knew he was due back in the U.S. in a few months, but I wasn't sure where he would be located.

Our visit to Alabama was over, and we had packed the car to come home. We went by his son's home to pick up his grandson. I was so upset because I wondered how Jacob was going to take care of me after my rotator cuff surgery and assist his grandson with obtaining employment.

We arrived in Orlando safely, and there were so many mixed feelings about how everything was going to work out. I just prayed because everything was totally out of my hands.

I was feeling so low down. Depression set in, and I cried, but I knew that "Weeping may endure for a night, but joy cometh in the morning." Psalm 30:5 KJV

I kept myself together and continued my therapist appointments.

My therapist could tell something was really wrong with me just by my mannerism and the way I greeted her. Thanks to my God and my therapist, I was (in the words of my parents and grandparents) kept "Clothed, in his right mind." Mark 5:15 KJV

Now, as a mature adult, I know for myself the true meaning of this phrase and the value of being so.

Lack of Consideration

Jacob proved over and over again that when it came to his family, he was untouchable. He continued to leave me out of the communication and decisions. He took his grandson to find a car. They found a nice one that cost seven thousand dollars. Jacob paid cash for it. Then, he told me his grandson was going to pay him back in increments.

Based on past experiences, I knew that wasn't going to happen. The grandson searched for jobs online. He was called to interview for a few of them. Finally, he landed a job at the Orlando airport with a contractor.

I was extremely proud of him. He left the house each morning dressed in his uniform. He was hard working on his job and did chores around our home to help Jacob and me. I was thankful and grateful.

He had child support issues, so his paycheck was short. He wasn't married but still was responsible for taking care of his two children. I could see that he was trying to be responsible and that he loved and cared about his grandfather.

Jacob had other grandchildren with whom he was not in a good relationship. I did not understand the dysfunction of it all; so, it was best for me was to leave it to God.

The grandson that was staying with us smoked and Jacob knew this before he invited him down to stay with us. I was a 14-year breast cancer survivor who had never smoked nor been around secondhand smoke.

When his grandson would come into the house from work, I could immediately smell the cigarette smoke, and I mentioned this to Jacob right away. I asked him to ask his grandson to take his clothes off right away, to shower, and to place his clothes in a trash bag in a laundry hamper I had placed in his bedroom.

He complied, but I could still smell the smoke because my body was literally sensitive to cigarette smoke. We decided to move the trash bags and his laundry to the laundry room, so he could wash the clothes every few days. At least, I thought this would help the smoke situation.

Bedside Manner

My rotator cuff surgery for my left shoulder was scheduled for May 7th. I had dreaded this surgery because I was a person who was very sensitive to pain medication like my mother was. Mother could only take Tylenol, and the same was true for me.

The surgery went well, and I was so glad that a girlfriend who lived here in Orlando had let me use her recliner when Jacob had his surgery. It was still in our home, and I would need it too.

My Orthopedic Surgeon had already made me aware that I would take more time to heal from the surgery because of Polymyositis disease. I was told that it was in my best interest to follow his instructions very carefully.

Jacob was there with me during the surgery.

When I came home from the hospital, I quickly realized that the recliner was going to be my best friend. I was in extreme pain. I was given opioids but taking them made it impossible for me to get up out of the recliner or to walk without Jacob's assistance.

Because of my sensitivity to the drugs, I would hallucinate and walk into walls.

I read the label information for the first drug they prescribed, Oxycodone. This was a dangerous drug. The label warning gave instructions on what to do if the patient was found not breathing.

I said to Jacob, "I am not taking this drug. If I take it and you are asleep, how will you know I'm unconscious?"

I did not take one single pill. I did not even bother to open the bottle. Instead, I placed a call to my surgeon's nurse, and they prescribed Hydrocodone, which also made me feel crazy. I completely stopped the opioid drugs and began taking Tylenol as directed every 6 hours. I was in extreme pain, but I just had to bear it.

The recliner was near the bed, where Jacob slept in our master suite. It was in front of the TV and the AC vent. Since I was so sensitive to smoke, I could smell it through the vent. Either the grandson wasn't putting his clothes in the hamper as instructed, or he was using a vapor cigarette in the house.

I could not find out because I was not able to climb the stairs to the second floor of our home. This was a huge problem, and consequently, I ended up with asthma. I literally could not breathe. I had to go to my Primary Care Physician.

"Remove whatever is causing the problem," he told Jacob.

This was the same thing my Allergist and Pulmonologist had said. They recommended that I "relocate immediately."

I was prescribed a Nebulizer machine with albuterol every 4 hours and Symbicort. My Primary Care Physician prescribed me a ProAir inhaler to keep with me in my purse at all times and an Epi-Pen (Epinephrine Injection) for allergic reactions if I encountered smoke from another person. I was told it could save my life.

I was worried. I was in so much pain every single day and relied heavily on Jacob. I could tell he was becoming exhausted from helping his grandson and me.

I had seen this coming, but Jacob had taken it lightly. His focus was on his grandson and ensuring he do better in life.

It was why I had suggested that Jacob wait until I healed from my surgery before his grandson came. But once again, Jacob refused to listen. He NEVER listened to me. At this point, our marriage was going further downhill and began to spiral out of control faster.

At night when I needed to go to the restroom, I would call Jacob to help me. But he would lie there in the bed and pretend he did not hear me. I would try multiple times calling out to him.

I had to go, and if I didn't get there soon, I would urinate on myself. I cried as I struggled to get out of the chair the best I could. I was trying to be careful, so I wouldn't fall.

It was so painful that now as I type these words, the tears are falling.

I begged God, "Please," I cried, "Please help me!"

I don't know why Jacob behaved the way he did toward me. I was in this particular situation because I had helped him when he had heart surgery. We had taken vows in front of God to be there for each other through sickness and in health.

Instead, Jacob turned the other cheek. His bedside manner was horrible, but I knew that was the work of Satan.

Gaining Independence

I desperately wanted to get better so that I could be independent enough to do the things I needed to do for myself.

Jacob would fix me light food because I did not feel like eating most of the time. There were so many problems on my mind.

There were days I didn't feel well enough to drive myself to my appointments, and Jacob wouldn't take me. I would have to find the strength to drive myself. I drove 40 miles an hour, but I made it.

Again, as I recall these memories, I am crying all over again. Emotional abuse is real. You may be able to hide it on the outside, but inside it will literally kill your soul and alter your mental health status.

There was one time I had asked Jacob to take me to Ollie's. The store carried a Bible my sister, Bernice, had told me about. I had others my siblings had given me, but I wanted this one as well. Reading the Bible was one thing that helped me to stay encouraged during these daily trials and tribulations.

Jacob dropped me off curbside, and I had my cane with me. Once he pulled off to park, I tried stepping up on the sidewalk, and my legs went out. I felt myself falling. I did my best not to fall on my left shoulder, which was in a full sling from surgery. I fell, and people came running up to me to make sure I was alright. By this time,

Jacob saw what had happened, and he began to run towards me.

There were other men there with Jacob, helping me get up off the cement walkway. I scarred my knee pretty badly and still have the scar today.

There were many days I felt like giving up, but my only son was the reason I kept going. I hadn't told him that I had surgery. We kept in contact through the WhatsApp. I'm sure he knew something was wrong, but I didn't want to discuss my personal problems with my son.

Instead, I talked to the Lord and to my therapist. I told her all the things that were going on with Jacob and me, and she informed me that my marriage was exacerbating my health.

When I was finally healed enough to attend Physical Therapy, it was unbearably painful. But what hurt more was that I knew deep down in my heart that while Jacob took me to my appointments, he did not want to.

Jacob was consistently changing for the worst, and he was NOT the SAME MAN I MARRIED! I felt in my heart I was heading for another divorce, and I was doing everything in my power, even at the expense of losing my health, to stay married to this man whom I no longer knew as a husband.

Watch Care

I requested from our pastor to attend another church under "Watch Care." I knew I had to divide myself away from Jacob so God to lead me in the right direction. I knew in my heart that divorce was coming. I just did not know when it would happen.

In the meantime, I kept my faith strong in the Lord and kept a smile on my face because God said, "I would never leave thee nor forsake thee." Hebrews 13:5 KJV

And I knew that He wouldn't and that my deliverance would come in His time, not mine.

Jacob's reason for leaving me when I needed him most was that he "needed a break." He didn't seem to care or understand that my current predicament was caused first by me lifting him and made worse by his grandson's smoking.

It was clear that my well-being was of no concern to Jacob. He was very selfish and lacked empathy. He had become a heartless individual whom I no longer knew as my husband.

He continued to leave me on a daily basis and stopped doing the things that he knew I enjoyed. I felt he resented me and was punishing me because I had left my jobs. Instead of telling me the truth, he found trivial things to find fault over, like the house not being clean.

He always tried to make me feel belittled by his sarcastic comments.

I recall a time Jacob left to take a break while I continued to struggle to stay alive. I had had enough, and I told God, "If you let me live to see Monday, I will be divorcing this man because at this point, I no longer consider him my husband."

I almost didn't live to see Monday!

When Jacob and his oldest son would travel for one of their trips, his son would generally park his car by our mailbox. This particular time, the car was not there, so I assumed Jacob picked him up at his home.

Later that night, as I was preparing to go to bed, I noticed the house was smelling like gas. I knew we did not have a gas stove, but there was a gas tank on the grill out on the lanai. I checked that tank immediately, and it was fine.

I walked to the back door of our home and opened the door that led to the garage. The smell of gas almost took my breath away. That's when

I realized Jacob's son had parked his car in the garage in Jacob's spot.

I ran back to my bedroom, called 911, and explained what was going on. They immediately connected me to our nearest fire station. The fireman instructed me they had my location. They said to hang up the phone, go outside, and get as far away from the house, NOW!

My phone could have ignited a fire!

I did as I was instructed and left my front door wide open. All I had on was my nightgown and house slippers. I was so scared. I didn't know what was going to happen. The firearm alarms were screaming loudly. I made sure I followed the fireman's instructions and made my way far from our home.

The firemen arrived and asked what happened. I told them that my son left his car in the garage and that he and his father were gone on a trip. He asked for the car keys, but I did not have any keys. The firemen went into the house where I left the front door open. They opened the garage and pushed the car away from the home and back into the cul de sac.

The fireman let up all the windows on the top floor because the bottom floor windows were locked down for security measures by our alarm system when it was installed. They opened the sliding doors in my master suite bedroom and also the sliding doors in the family room, which led to the lanai and pool areas.

As I recall this incident, I realize that my Father God had me covered and protected from all harm and danger that may have been meant for me.

"What A Mighty God We Serve!" (Original Writer Unknown)

Conclusion

I did live to see Monday as God saw fit for His child, and I called the best attorney in town. I knew about her through an acquaintance.

"My husband has a great attorney," she said.

"If it's not too personal," I began, "May I have her name?"

She gave me the information, and I realized her office was located close to where I went for my hair appointments.

I called Women's Family Law Firm and spoke with Christina M, Green, Esq. The website said she was an Attorney, a Mediator, and a Parenting Coordinator. Her motto was "Putting Your Family First."

Attorney Green only had one appointment for a consultation that day, and it was at 2 pm. I immediately scheduled it. This appointment was for me!

I arrived at her office and felt at ease with her right away. I explained my situation and told her

I wanted her to handle my divorce. I felt reassured knowing that everything we spoke about from the time we signed a contract would be confidential.

She assured me that she had my best interest in mind and would from the beginning to the end.

During our first session, I was so torn and broken.

She did ask me directly, "Are you sure you are ready to move forward?"

"Yes," I replied. And I was.

I filed for divorce in the month of August but became gravely ill due to all the stress with my health and personal life.

My illness had exacerbated. It was a month later, in September, before I finally filed for divorce from Jacob.

In my heart and soul, I knew I could no longer take the emotional abuse from him. Even though our marriage began as a fairytale (especially our wedding), four of my specialists had written a letter indicating that I needed to relocate.

In other words, they were asking me, "Do you wish to stay and die or relocate and become better with your health?"

This was a no brainer; I WANTED TO LIVE!

Fear

As I reflect now on my life with Jacob, I should have departed sooner, but I was trying my best to uphold the vows we took, which Jacob seem to have quickly forgotten.

Jacob was actually a piece of work, and as I look back on our marriage, I can see why we both had previously failed marriages.

For me, I was always trying to abide by what God would have wanted me to do. I know now that marriage is a partnership and takes three people to be successful: you, your spouse, and God. If either one of these is missing, you will be in trouble.

If you are reading this and have gone through some things or are still in some things, allow me to give you a piece of advice. Do not let fear paralyze you. Don't be afraid of what people may say about you.

Even if everyone turns against you, know that Jesus Christ will never leave nor forsake you in way, shape, or form. If you place your total trust in Him, He won't let you down.

There will be a lot of people who will judge me for writing what they consider a "Tell All" book, but I'm not afraid of them or what they have to say.

The Way Out

During this 2020 Pandemic, God has molded me (and is still molding me) into the masterpiece in which He would have me to be. I am a bold soldier for the Lord. He gave me battles to fight along the way and the strength to do so. I have survived to give my written testimony so that others may know there is help to be had.

If you think there is no way out, I am here to tell you that the Bible is full of ways out. Read the Bible. Live by the scriptures, and don't "act" like a Christian, "be" a Christian.

When you grow in intimacy with God, He will direct your path. You just have to continue praying regardless of your circumstances because our Father God will never fail you. As the saying goes, *"He may not come when YOU want Him to; however, GOD is always on time."*

When I talk about "the goodness of Jesus and all He has done for me, my soul cries out Hallelujah, and I thank God for saving me." (Bishop G. E. Patterson)

I am not afraid to tell anyone that in addition to prayer, get mental health checkups. We know what God can do when we talk to Him; however, remember this: God gave talent and skills to each one of us, including physicians.

Purpose

Do you know your purpose for living? Do you know that you have one? Ask God, "What is my life's purpose?"

Life is not just about living but is also about thriving and giving back to others. Giving does not always have to be monetary; it can be giving of your God-given talent.

You may not discover this right away, which is why it is so important to have an intimate relationship with God *and* to spend time with a psychologist. In my opinion, this is an issue within the Black community. YES, I am saying this because there are statistics to back me up. Just google the subject for yourself. You can also go to the library if you don't have access to a computer or cellular device. Please do the research.

Emotional Abuse

I am making one statement from the bottom of my heart is to the people who are going to judge me for the things I disclosed about my marriage. I knew Jacob for a year before we dated. I dated him for a year and was married to him for 13. Unless you lived with this man in our home, you don't know him as I know him. Yes, you may know him as a friend, father, uncle, cousin, or whatever, but not as my husband. No one knows what went on in our home but Jacob, Jesus, and me.

I am not perfect by any means, and we all have flaws. However, there are certain things in this life that, while they may be invisible to the outside world, they are very real and harmful for you. Emotional abuse, like certain illnesses that can't always be seen, can be very harmful and devastating to your life.

If you are dealing with abuse of any kind, please seek mental health treatment or be advised by a counselor immediately.

I came home one day, and there was a letter lying on the table.

I prayed before I opened it. I quickly scanned the letter and saw the words "Fully Favorable." I had been approved for my disability, which was something I'd had to fight for as well.

Again, I'm crying as I recount this story because so much of my struggle has been because people didn't "see" the pain of my life. They couldn't see my aches, fears, and torments. So, they decided my ailments didn't exist.

If you only look at me from the outside, you have NO idea what I'm dealing with on the inside. I struggle to maintain my health.

I have been ridiculed, talked about, belittled, and discounted all because my pain isn't visible to the outside world. My pain is invisible and incurable.

Fully Favorable

Even now, I pray to God, asking Him to continue to help me through these times, which I'm told I'll have to live with for the rest of my life.

And although it is frustrating that people judge me by what I look like, I'm grateful that I don't look like what I'm going through!

I can keep a smile on my face every day regardless of my circumstances.

With the letter in my hand, I walked over to where Jacob was sitting on the couch. He had his legs on the chair and his hands behind his head.

I sat in the recliner next to him.

"You never believed I was sick," I said, crying once more. "But the Judge says I am and has approved my disability. The judge says I am sick with many invisible, incurable diseases."

Jacob just sat there.

"Today," I continued, "I FILED FOR DIVORCE FROM YOU!"

Then, I got up from the edge of the recliner, still crying, and went to my bedroom.

My emotions were high. It was only by the grace of God that on the day, I was well enough to file for divorce. I received my disability approval letter.

I think God was waiting on me to take the first step. This was my destiny. He did not want His child to continue to suffer emotional abuse. He provided a way out.

A Masterpiece

My attorney notified me that Jacob waived his rights to appear in court.

My first thought was, "An emotional abuser is a COWARD!"

Jacob didn't want to face his reality. He knew he was the problem. I went to court with God on my side because I had held up my marriage vows, and I had no guilt within my soul.

The divorce was finalized, and I grieved a second marriage.

I had no idea it would happen this way.

One thing I've learned as I've fought one battle after another is that you have to accept what you cannot change.

I can't tell you that the ending of my second marriage wasn't painful because it was then and still is now.

As I tell my story and relive the horror of it all, I can't stop crying. The pain of being beaten down emotionally is indescribable on its own, but even more so when you are dealing with physical pain. I was left alone to suffer and wonder how I was going to do the things I needed to do.

This next thing I'm about to say is so very important:

We must stop judging people. Unless you walk in another person's shoes, you can't possibly know how they are feeling.

I've decided to use my story and my pain to be an advocate for those who haven't found their voices.

Through my non-profit, I'm in touch with so many people who share their stories with me about how they are coping. I realize that the first step in helping them is making sure others know that abuse of any kind is wrong and that if you are being abused, there is help for you.

At this point in my life, I am better mentally, physically, and spiritually.

I know God is not done with me. This is just the beginning.

I was **broken,** but I did not **break**.

I am still God's masterpiece, being groomed, shaped, and molded into what He would have me to be.

Bonus Chapter: My Son

Sports

My first husband, Peter and I were both were very busy working and taking care of the home. Even still, enjoying family time was important to us.

One thing we all enjoyed was attending our son's sports activities on Saturday mornings.

Abel kept us busy!

He played every sport beginning with T-ball when he was just five years old. He also had a love for baseball, basketball, and football.

We were worn out as parents, but seeing our son happy was most important for us. Sports helped our son's personality and encouraged him to be social at a young age. We were pleased with that.

Abel loved people and was outgoing like his father. Jacob played basketball as an adult sport, and Abel would go with him each time their league played on Saturday. I didn't let him go during the week because he had homework to complete.

Our son enjoyed going to school; however, he did not like completing his homework. When he didn't finish it, we would ground him from visiting with his friends in the neighborhood, playing video games, or going outside to swim in our pool.

Abel loved to swim. We knew right away that the expense of having one installed in our backyard was well worth it.

The pool was beautiful.

It was 8 feet on one end, 3 feet on the other, and had a diving board. There was even a hand bar into the pool and a pool shower! I must say *Parnell Pools* in Fayetteville, North Carolina did an outstanding job with our pool installation.

Abel had learned to swim at an early age at Hillcrest Daycare. He went to preschool there, and the owner had a pool at the daycare school, which was wonderful for the children who wished to learn how to swim.

As parents, we eagerly signed the authorization form for our son to learn how to swim. Because he was so young, he was fearless and soon swam like a fish. For a child his age, he was an excellent swimmer.

Academics

I learned that one reason my son didn't care much for homework was that he was not a strong student. He didn't learn as easily as other children. Abel was a visual learner, so on some tests, for example, he did not perform very well.

Thankfully we learned this early on during his elementary years as a result of attending parent-teacher conferences and reviewing progress reports.

During this time, his teachers were exceptional in working with him. I also placed him in tutoring classes in his afterschool program, which worked out very well.

He would pass with lower grades than I wanted him to have, and as his mother, I knew he had the potential to do better. He just wasn't placing all his efforts into school.

Sports were always on his mind, so when high school was on the horizon, that was how I finally got his attention.

"If your grades are not good, you cannot play sports," I informed my son.

I knew this would motivate him to display his best efforts. He would need to do his homework, turn his homework back into his teacher as instructed, and follow direct instructions at all times if he wished to make the team. He would also have to maintain those grades if he wanted to remain on the team every quarter.

My plan worked!

My son was adapting to high school. In the beginning, it was somewhat cumbersome. We both were adjusting to his new schedule: school, football practice, and making sure that he completed his homework.

It was also important to me that he has time to have fun with this friends and peers. Abel was such a lovable kid.

The Village

I felt bad sometimes that he had to take on more responsibility at an earlier age now that I was a single parent. But it was necessary. I had to work to make sure we had what we needed.

When I had to work later or to work overtime, my son was with his Godparents, Thomas, Sr. and Feary McKethan, and his Godbrother, "T." "T" and Abel had a brotherly bond. This was true for his other Godbrother, Ron. As a matter of fact, to this day, they are inseparable.

As young boys, they kept their discussions between themselves unless their funds were running low. Then, they quickly involved us parents in their plans hoping we would help them out with cash.

My son enjoyed going to church because of the youth activities, but Sunday morning was a different story.

I made him get up and go anyway. I knew we both needed to attend, and I instilled the Word of God in him because it was a high priority.

Through the week, if there were church activities, I definitely could depend on my friends, James and Linda to get him there. Their son and my son were around the same age, which worked out great. The boys were as close as real brothers.

My neighbors were my saving grace when I needed them to pick up Abel or to take him somewhere for me.

We remain friends to this day, and I say that was "God's Intervention." He knew I would need help when my marriage ended.

Preparing for College

As Abel continued high school, he still exhibited difficulty in learning. He seemed to be struggling. I spoke with his teachers individually at Parent-Teacher Conferences to see how he was doing in their classes. I didn't want to just rely on a progress report or a report card. I reviewed the grades; however, I wanted to know how his interactions in the classroom were.

I learned he would be looking out the window, daydreaming, would not sit in any chair during the entire class, and did not complete his tasks on time during class.

I felt he needed an Individual Educational Plan (IEP).

A few weeks later, I met this wonderful, soft-spoken, caring teacher who was very familiar with students like Abel. I was relieved in a sense to know someone was able to assist my son and to provide the proper learning techniques that would cater to his style of learning and understanding. He was doing the best he could with the tools he had. He needed new and better tools.

I did not wish my son to be labeled as a slow learner. If this occurred, his college admission would be almost impossible. But now, thanks to Ms. Barbara, Abel was heading in the right direction.

We learned that multiple-choice questions were better for Abel than responding to essay type questions. At Ms. Barbara's suggestion, he attended both smaller classes as well as others on his grade level.

His hard work paid off, and he made the football team. He was delighted to tell me once I was home from work. We both were excited. This was a greater responsibility for me as a single parent. However, at this point, I would do anything for my son to be happy. I knew that with the help of God, I would be able to do just that.

My son's last year of high school was difficult and puzzling for me as a parent. There was one teacher (his geometry teacher) who was more than what I could understand or comprehend. It seemed she had no compassion or understanding for students who learned differently.

How could such a person be allowed to teach?

Abel needed this Geometry class to graduate from high school.

I had to meet with her quite often to ensure my son was meeting the curriculum of her class. Eventually, the IEP got involved in this grave concern of mine about her teaching process of IEP students.

I did what I had to do for my son. It was what my parents demonstrated for my siblings and me. My background was so very different from Peter's, and I'm certain that is why when I needed him, he wasn't there. It was devastating and hard to believe this teacher's lack of empathy for her students.

Nothing and no one was going to stop me from preparing my son for a successful life.

The Short Term/Long Term Lesson

My son didn't see very much of his father because of his after-school activities. I felt like if his father wanted to see him play or practice, he would make his way to the high school to spend time with his son there.

Abel was disappointed, but he didn't let that stop him.

His grades continued to improve, and he remained on the football field.

I'll never forget the night he was injured.

I saw him fall and knew he was in pain. I got up and ran onto the field. The office tried to stop me, but I yelled, "That is my son!"

The adrenaline was pumping inside me, and thankfully, the office let me through.

At that point, I didn't care if they had fined me with a cost at the courthouse. Seeing my son lying there on the ground in obvious pain was all I cared about, and I would have done anything to get to him.

The coach and medical team had him surrounded. They told him not to move until he was told to do so and began asking him questions trying to determine what was wrong.

"I feel like my ankle is broken," Abel said.

I worked hard to keep my face straight and not cry.

Abel's face was covered in pain, and that broke my heart.

He refused to get on a stretcher. He wanted to be brave. With the coach and medical team assisting him, he walked off the field. The crowd gave him great applause, and that's when I began to tear up.

Abel was a man in spite of his father's absence. I was so proud.

They told me to meet them at the ambulance that was on standby. They were transporting him to the hospital.

Once we reached the Emergency Room at Cape Fear Valley Medical Center, my son, one of the football team staff, and I went back to see the Emergency Physician immediately. X-rays revealed that his ankle was fractured, and the Orthopedic Physician on call was called to the Emergency Room.

He examined my son, reviewed the x-rays, and informed us that Abel's ankle was indeed fractured. He was going to place a cast on it, and we would need to make an appointment the following week.

My son was prescribed pain medication and crutches. He was so disappointed that he would not be playing football.

Once we made it home, he was still very frustrated and in pain. I gave him a lot of compassion and let him know he was going to be alright.

"Six to eight weeks isn't a long time at all," I said, hoping to encourage him. "Before you know it, you'll be back on the football field."

I let him know that he could still go sit on the sideline and support his teammates. He was so much better once I sat and talked to him about the short term versus longtime effects of his fractured ankle.

My son's doctor was exceptional. He kept Abel encouraged and gave him home exercises to do. And in what seemed like no time, Abel was healed.

In my opinion, what helped him heal the most was the fact that he was able to see his football team play from the sideline. It didn't matter to him if they won or lost; he was happy to be there.

He still was maintaining his grades at an acceptable level, and I was good with the IEP he had with Ms. Barbara. The IEP plan was working in his other classes too.

My son was able to return to the team to play. It was a gradual process. The coach was great in assisting my son while being mindful of his health.

Sense of Normalcy

I was concerned about how my son would survive our divorce.

Would he thrive, or would he suffer from our failure?

I worked hard to make our routine as normal as possible. I wanted him to experience everything he would have if his father had still been in our home.

So, when it was time, Abel learned to drive. He got his license, and I bought him a *hooptee* car for $600 from an elderly Caucasian man. The car was in good condition and ran very well. It had a lot of miles on it, but it afforded Abel's transportation.

It was good for me too because I didn't have to take him everywhere anymore. With more privileges came more responsibilities.

The rules were that no one could ride with him except his Godbrothers. The deal was if he broke that agreement, I would take the car away for a week. I trusted him to do the right thing because he had also been told that if he did well with this vehicle, he would be rewarded with a new vehicle.

Along with the boundaries, Abel also had to work because he was responsible for keeping gas in his car, getting the oil changed, and providing his own lunch money. I would take care of everything else.

Abel got a job and throughout high school, working weekends at Kentucky Fried Chicken and Hardee's (which he despised, but I did not let him quit). He moved on to the Cross Creek Mall and got a job at Finish Line as a salesperson. He loved that job because he was able to talk to people. He also worked at Foot Locker/Foot Action. My son seemed to enjoy his jobs at these locations inside the mall area. He also was assigned the stock room when the inventory of shoes arrived.

I know he enjoyed the extra freedom and felt good about shouldering some of his responsibilities. However, I had to remember he was still a teenager.

A parent told me that they saw three boys in my son's car. When I asked him about it, he told me the truth.

I was happy he was truthful, but one thing I had to teach him was consequences. I took the car for a week, and yes, it was definitely a lesson learned.

When he had to catch a ride with another friend, he quickly went back to the rules that were set in place.

Aside from that mishap, Abel drove and behaved responsibly with his car. So, I kept my word and purchased him a brand new, black Rodeo.

I remember the day like it was yesterday.

When I drove up to the house driving the truck, Abel ran out to meet me. When I told him it was his, he began to jump up and down and thanked God!

I don't know who was happier that day, him or me. I was so happy to be able to give my son something special and something he had earned.

Independence

After witnessing how Jacob interacted with his children and how one of his sons had a family of his own but continuously needed help, I was more than grateful for Abel.

As a kid, Abel had a lot of independence, and that worried me sometimes. He would hang out with his friends, go to movies, and do things that teenagers did.

But I always reminded him, "Please do not get into any trouble. If you see any trouble, immediately leave."

His father and I both said, "If you get in any trouble, you are going to stay in jail, and we will not bail you out!"

Who knows if we would have actually done that? Still, we wanted to plant this incentive to stay out of trouble in his mind early. Abel remembers this vividly to this day.

I'm so thankful his father and I never had to see if we had the stomach to leave our child in a jail cell!

Lessons

Now that my son is grown, he and I reminisce about the old days from time to time.

Things were hard, but I don't think I'd change anything.

Through the adversity, both of us have grown stronger.

I'm happy that I made sure he kept up with his studies. Abel was taught the value of things, and when he made bad choices, it was important for me to teach him consequences.

I know growing up without his father in the home was hard for him. It was hard for both of us but having that extra responsibility has served him in his adult life. My son works hard and is respected for his job. He has done very well for himself.

He is my pride and joy. I love him dearly, and I thank God for giving me such a wonderful, kind, and caring young man to call son.

About the Author

After many years of serving others in the medical field, Author Miyoshi Umeki Gordon found herself in need of essential medical care. Diagnosed with myositis and breast cancer, the author felt broken and wondered how she would ever survive what she calls multiple unknown illnesses.

In addition to the incurable physical diseases in her body, the author was also battling emotional abuse and the effects of living with a drug addict (her first husband). However, with all the battles placed upon her by life, she never gave up on herself. For her, God was (and remains) at the forefront of her life.

With what can only be credited to the grace of God, the Campbell University Cum Laude graduate not only survived but emerged with a renewed sense of purpose. Her renewed passion for helping others compelled her to come out of retirement and launch a 501(c)(3) nonprofit organization.

As the author reassembles her life into God's masterpiece, she desires to assist others who silently suffer from the physical and emotional trauma that threatens their life's purpose.

Miyoshi has one adult son.

You may contact the author on social media:

- Facebook: Author Miyoshi Gordon
- Instagram: @authormiyoshigordon
- Twitter: @GordonMiyoshi
- Website: united-adivinepurposeinc.com

Helpful Resources

American Cancer Society

Susan G. Komen

National Breast Cancer Foundation

Breast Cancer Research Foundation

Living Beyond Breast Cancer (LBBC)

The Myositis Association (TMA)

Autoimmune Related Disease Association

National Domestic Violence Hotline: 1-800-799-7233

Domestic Violence Immediate Help: Dial 911

National Coalition Against Domestic Violence (NCADV)

Mayo Clinic

Duke University Medical Center

John Hopkins Myositis Center

Arthritis Foundation

Cure Juvenile Myositis Foundation

National Organization for Rare Disorders

Raynaud's Association

Centers for Disease Control and Prevention

World Health Organization

National Institute of Health

Mental Health America

National Alliance on Mental Illness (NAMI)

National Institute of Mental Health – (NIH)

National Mental Health Association

National Council for Behavioral Health

The Boris Lawrence Henson Foundation – Mental Health

the Butterfly Typeface

Made in the USA
Columbia, SC
17 November 2020